W9-ABB-253

PRAISE FOR
*WAITING FOR OUR SOULS
TO CATCH UP*

"Sister Carol Perry is one of the most brilliant biblical scholars I have ever known. She truly breaks the mold: a loyal Roman Catholic who marches ahead of and challenges her denomination in much of the world's social agenda, a respected nun who has been on the staff of America's oldest Protestant congregation for over 30 years, and a woman of maturity who holds an undeniable appeal to the young and the hip. When you read this book, you are in for a treat. It will leave you longing for more."

— Michael Brown
Senior Minister
Marble Collegiate Church

"Bring your highlighter and your sense of wonder to a comfortable chair and marvel at what you didn't know about Biblical history. *Waiting For Our Souls To Catch Up* is a must read for all those seeking a spiritual peace in a high-tech world. But most of all bring your appreciation of Sister Carol Perry's scholarly brilliance in refining prayer, faith, and grace. I love this book. I will always have two, my annotated one and another one to give away."

— Rolland G. Smith
Broadcast journalist, author, and poet

ALSO BY CAROL M. PERRY, SU

Called and Sent: A Brief History of the Society of Saint Ursula
(with Agnes McManus, SU)

WAITING FOR OUR SOULS TO CATCH UP

~~~~~

Reason, Ritual, and Faith in
Our Fallow Time

~~~~~

CAROL M. PERRY, SU

Asahina and Wallace
Los Angeles
2014
http://www.asahinaandwallace.com

Copyright © 2014 by Carol M. Perry, SU

Published in the United States by Asahina & Wallace, Inc. (http://www.asahinaandwallace.com)

ISBN: 978-1-940412-10-8

Library of Congress Control Number: 2014935119

Table of Contents

WITH MUCH GRATITUDE TO
ALL THOSE WHO BELIEVED
IT COULD BE AND WHO SAID SO

BEFORE BEGINNING...

NOT ONE OF US had a choice about being born, nor did we choose either the country of our birth or the historical era in which we were to take root. But after our arrival here, life becomes more and more complex as we face an endless series of choices.

Things are made no simpler since we are living in what social scientists delight in calling a "paradigm shift," one of those moments in which everything we once held as firmly given begins to move beyond our control. It is as if we took a wrong turn on the yellow brick road and landed in a very strange Oz. We are caught up in the digital world.

How many objects do you possess that your grandparents would not recognize? We have an ever-growing vocabulary of smartphones, Kindles, Nooks, and laptops, to say nothing of apps and iPads and...

In every way, our lives have been changed by technology. People use phones not to speak to others, but to send text messages to them. Office workers interact with others continents away. The virtual college experience is increasingly common. Banking needs are met without human interaction. Restaurants present the intriguing sight of two people dining together while their fingers keep up social contact with someone far from the table.

High-school students struggle to get to class; many of them are fatigued not because they were up late writing a paper, but because they were on the Web, which knows no schedule. Psychologists now list Internet Use Disorder as a new mental ailment. One recent study found that the brains of Internet addicts begin to resemble those of cocaine addicts or alcoholics.

This is our world, a place where we feel almost naked when we are temporarily cut off from our devices. This is our world, where we go on vacation and take the office with us. This is our world, where the nearest Starbucks is filled with people who do not speak to each other, but who connect to distant worlds.

Has the thought of having a spiritual journey in this strange new existence occurred to you? If so, to ask the question is actually to begin the process, although we wonder how to set out.

One place is to consider some of the most obvious questions about the spiritual self and its problems, those puzzling issues that keep cropping up in the mind of a thinking person. Then we might want to look at the Bible and how it might figure in our journey. It seems to belong, yet it is cloaked in mystery.

Shall we start?

~ 1 ~

"MY DAYS ARE A HEADLONG DASH FROM THING TO THING! HOW CAN I FIND TIME FOR A SPIRITUAL LIFE? HELP!"

WHAT DO WE MOST WANT? Our honest answer might be: more time. If we never seem to get everything done, something has to be put on hold. That something is too often our soul's care.

While we might not have put our dilemma into just those words, many of us do often feel harried and in need of something that eludes our grasp. The more cynical among us might see it as a kind of betrayal by some of the institutions we once relied on to support us.

Our political system has devolved into bitter partisanship, with the public good a pale mirage. Our churches are often groping for their lost place in our culture. And our schools have become so test-results-driven that the idea of the "joy of learning" might evoke a bitter chuckle.

Too bleak a picture? Put like that, it is, but each of these contributes to our personal and social dis-ease. We have a hunger for the more. Is there a way to satisfy that hunger?

I love the story of the two Englishmen who were exploring in the heart of Africa in the 19th century. So engrossed were they in their adventures that the calendar escaped them until they realized that they had a very limited time to get to the port on the nearest coast before a steamer would leave for England. If they missed it, weeks would elapse before the next one would dock.

In haste, they packed up their camp and called their native porters to shoulder the baggage. Off they set at a goodly clip. One day, two days passed, and they were nearing the coast. But on day three, as the explorers clapped their hands for everyone to set out again, the bearers refused to rise from beneath the trees. Their spokesperson explained, "We have been going too fast. We must stay here and wait for our souls to catch up with us."

Myth or fact, the story makes a profound point. We moderns have long ago left our vital spiritual component somewhere in a jungle clearing. Do we wonder why we are so frazzled?

There are little ways by which we can reclaim this vital part of who we are and in the process better understand how and why we are. We agree that we do not have enough time for reflection. We agree that our calendars are overloaded. But that does not mean that there is no place for God in our lives.

I often begin simply at the start of a new month or new season by blessing my instruments of work. You could do the same. Bless the phone so that the words you say might be good and helpful ones. Say a prayer over the computer for the work you and it will do together. Since I know that the office copier has a prejudice against me, I often bless it before I press the *on* button.

These little rituals need not be witnessed by anyone else. They are simply a way of claiming what we use so that all our uses might be lifted above the mundane. They apply equally well to cars and car keys, to kitchen utensils and home implements. We are then no longer alone in our sometimes frantic efforts. Instead, we are consciously asking God to share the load.

There is nothing that need escape our blessing fervor. Snap on the dog's leash with a prayer, attach the toddler's seatbelt with one, pick up the errant backpack with a blessing. Stretch it to cover the dishwasher and the washing machine, the vacuum, and the dust cloth. Our lists are uniquely ours, *bless the*

but the stuff of our lives suddenly acquires added value.

I like to think of this process as a way of making every day a holy day. Ordinary things become more than plastic and metal and bits of wire. They become invitations to our inner self to look beyond, and they take no time from our over-scheduled days. However, they do center us both within and without.

Now let's look at another aspect of our interconnectedness. I regularly meet groups of people for a lunchtime Bible study before they head back to their offices. Some of their frustrations might also be yours. One complaint is that they can never escape work since the boss can send email or text messages at will.

One of them said, "I no longer have a free day. Before I get home on Friday night, he has already sent things he wants done by Monday morning."

It is an exaggeration, but I sometimes think of an employer like this as a modern Simon Legree. How can we workers cope without losing our souls in the process?

We must give ourselves fallow time. Farmers long ago learned that fields must not be planted year after year with the same crop. Fertilizer has largely done away with

13

the practice of allowing the land to rest, but no one is yet advertising soul fertilizer. We have to make our own.

Mealtime can be soul time

Don't miss the natural renewal time: mealtime. We moderns are in grave danger of losing it completely as we eat on the run or multitask across our dinners.

Why not extend our blessings to food and all that is involved in even the simplest of meals? The coffee maker surely deserves a blessing. So many unseen, unknown hands have brought food to our kitchens, and our prayers can include them, too. Even the youngest members of the family can become aware that we live in an interrelated world. Others make our lives possible. It is a holy thought to be reminded of this.

Our ancestors respected food as the source of life. Food sharing was the time when they came together to share something else: the fabric of their lives. It was conversation time.

One thing that rarely happened in antiquity was sharing food with a stranger. A stranger in ancient Greece and Rome would eat apart until he was trusted enough to be welcomed into the family or clan. Once a stranger had broken bread with the group, he would never again be an enemy.

This is obvious in *The Odyssey*, where Odysseus and Telemachus, on separate journeys, are both welcomed as visitors by many rulers. They are always given the normal signs of hospitality — a bath, fresh clothing, and food at a small table apart. Then, and only then, are they asked who they are and how they might be in need. By the next meal they might be welcomed to the table with the household.

The Bible has a wonderfully similar story of the power of food, in Joshua 9. Israel has come into the Promised Land, and its first conquests have gone to its head. Over the hill lies the next victim, the town of Gibeon. Its clever inhabitants decide to save themselves. They dig out their oldest clothing, pack up a few crusts of dry bread, and go to meet Israel, spinning a yarn about having left home far away when their clothing was new and their bread fresh from the oven. They declare that they have come a long way in search of these new conquerors. They ask to enter into covenant with them.

Joshua and the elders fail to think this through, but promptly eat with these talespinners. They discover the ploy when it is too late. Food has been shared and the

Gibeonites are "in the family." They cannot be destroyed. Such is the power of food.

We need to recall this uniting power of food as we eat in haste, omit the dining room from plans for new houses, and, worse, not allow ourselves to relax with food. Meals are not a waste of time. They can give meaning to the time before and the time to come. Mealtime can be soul time.

You might also want to find other daily pauses to nourish you. Be daring and turn off that phone for an hour while you do whatever demands your full attention. Don't check your email every 15 minutes. Allow yourself the joy of walking from place to place without being plugged in. The world will not end.

We need to be unplugged long enough to notice who we are and where we are going. The constant noise in our ears leaves very little time for thoughts to be formulated or for our souls to taste what quiet might be like.

The new normal of this electronic age is a bit scary. Some of the overuse is due to the novelty of technology. It has a big downside, though, in the very trivializing of the shared word. Lovers' conversations and quarrels have become one-sided sharings with everyone else on the bus or subway platform.

Both tenderness and snide remarks are aired in the public arena. What is left for private conversation?

Reclaim and respect your private arena. Let your inner self breathe as you transition from one thing to another. Better yet, pray, the best of soul fertilizers.

How can we do that?

"What is prayer? Can I do it out of church? How does it differ from saying prayers, like the 'Our Father'?"

THE PROCESS OF PRAYING might seem daunting, but it is really quite simple. The best definition of prayer is the classic one: the lifting of the heart and mind to God. That need not be hard. We are God's creatures, standing on his good earth, and it is natural to acknowledge him.

I try to do this in more than one way. On my trek to the water cooler, I offer a prayer for the colleagues whose desks are on my route. Or I think of those on the floor below, and send a little spiritual thought to them. They haven't a clue that I am doing it, but my soul feels better for thinking of someone beside myself.

I have other little prayer moments that lift me from the relentless self-absorption that is part of human nature. When I squeeze into the subway to get to work, I try to pray for those traveling with me. If I can glance down the car, I do so, mentally noting the woman with the small child, the man with his mop and bucket (yes, I have ridden with him), the student struggling to get her homework finished, the woman already tired with her eyes closed … They each get a prayer for the day ahead.

If the train is too crowded to do more than hang on to my pole, I include them all in a global prayer that those of us traveling together might have a day that is good. I find that blessing those sharing space with me lets me view that space differently. It lifts me out of myself and allows someone else to enter in.

But we also need to pray in longer, more intentional times, or signs of spiritual starvation will become apparent. If you are serious about having a spiritual life, then you have to set aside time for prayer.

Prayer

Prayer is funny stuff, isn't it? The timid are afraid of the word, the desperate cling to the concept and either praise its success or stoutly deny that they ever believed it would work, the pious offer it as a remedy for every ill, and the realist acknowledges its power and its flaws. We are probably all included somewhere in that list.

Put simply, prayer is part of a relationship. If one believes in a personal deity, in a God who is more than a vague presence in the atmosphere — and I do — then we have to get to know that God.

Prayer is work, an exercise, a focusing on someone besides ourselves. We are born totally dependent creatures, having our every physical and emotional need met by someone else. About the age of two, we begin to assert our independence in ways that can be humorous. "Do it myself" results in mis-buttoned jackets and mittens on the wrong hands, but the determined little person is fiercely proud of his accomplishments.

We are no different in the world of the spirit. We want to be in charge, but, no matter how successful we might be, we will eventually find ourselves in a situation beyond our human control. So we cry out for help, often in a prayer of petition.

Petition is what most people think of when they hear the word "prayer." One of the more delightful examples of this kind of praying comes from a wonderfully holy priest I once knew. He had been to our convent for an early Mass on a sleety winter's morning. On his way home, his car spun out of control on a bridge and came to a stop against the guardrail, which bulged but held firm.

When later asked if he had thought to pray during that crucial moment, he said, "It occurred to me to pray, so I did. When the car stopped spinning, I heard myself desperately saying aloud, 'Bless us, O Lord, and these thy gifts which we are about to receive from thy bounty...'" It was the standard blessing before meals! The words were not a bad spontaneous choice.

Prayer, however, is more than just asking for things. Quite obviously, if God is God, then there is no need for our asking him for what he already knows we need. He doesn't need to hear us, but we need to hear ourselves. Putting our desires into words very often shapes those thoughts into something more real.

Let's go to the Gospels for an example, to the day when the disciples asked Jesus, "Teach us to pray." They were concerned that they were missing out on something. In his answer, Jesus was never more particularly Jewish nor more universal. He gave them the "Our Father." Look at its elements:

"Our Father" This acknowledges who God is and who he is in relation to us. In a patriarchal world, God is the only perfect father, the one who gives life and then cares for each family member no matter how far he or she might stray. Fatherhood cannot be undone. God wants us to use that personal pronoun *our*. He is mine and yours.

"Who art in Heaven" God is more than an earthly benefactor. He dwells beyond this earth, yet is forever tied to those he will one day welcome into his dwelling place, wherever that might be.

"Hallowed be thy name" Every ancient knew the power of a name. If one knew someone's name, then one had been admitted into a relationship. To know a name was to know something intimate and personal about that person, whose name was also descriptive of his or her nature. Therefore, if God's name is power and intimacy, it must be used with care.

"Thy kingdom come" We no longer live in a world divided into kingdoms, although they once defined the limits of earthly power. Here, the speaker confesses that God has a desire, as it were. God would like to rule the heart of every

human being, but we control our own borders. We permit or deny entry.

"Thy will by done..." This is a hard petition. Our human wills are our dearest expression of ourselves. This is the humble prayer that says we know we are not in sole charge of what occurs.

"Give us this day..." We would like God to take care of all future needs. God says: No, I'll take care of each day. It is a reminder of the manna in the desert, which the Israelites had to gather each day. Any zealous soul who thought to take care of tomorrow by storing the extra discovered he had gleaned something that turned useless overnight. This petition is a great call to live in the present moment, which is the only time we actually possess.

"Forgive us..." Here, we have to stop and listen to what we are saying. This is the hardest of all the petitions. If we really mean it, and God takes us at our word, we could be in deep trouble. We go on to say, *"Forgive us as we forgive..."* That tricky little "as" can be such a judgment we impose on ourselves. What grievances are we toting around, what little "get evens" would we love to

set in motion? This prayer says "no" to revenge.

"Lead us not into temptation..." ("Do not bring us to the time of trial...") Either translation asks that we be kept from the dangers that always lurk. Remember that Jesus was giving this prayer to his disciples, so they must have found some familiarity with its spirit. How many of the psalms reverberate here!

All prayer is an exercise. It has to be integrated into our daily living. In channel surfing recently, I came across an interview with an athlete who spoke of his regimen of daily training: "I cannot skip a day or I waste time on the following day trying to catch up. If I want to win, I must train every day." Three days later, I caught his triumph on the medal podium, and I realized how well he knew what he had to do to reach his goal.

Our lives run the gamut of needs and crises and so must our prayer experiences. Sometimes we pray out of the honest admission that we are not omnipotent. We frankly acknowledge our place as creatures in a world we neither create nor control. I would call such a prayer one of simple humility.

Sometimes we pray out of need. We face one of those imponderables of life — loss, sickness, a tangled relationship — and we need light for the journey, light we are not capable of generating by ourselves.

Sometimes we pray out of joy. The day is glorious, something very good has happened, love has touched us, and we want to say thanks. We did not make it happen, but we are glad that it did.

Do I believe that prayer changes situations? Without going down a complex theological path, I would like to simply suggest that prayer can often change our approach to the situation. It has the power to calm us down and to give us time to reflect. It also invites God to touch our lives.

I come to this topic prejudiced in favor of prayer, I admit, because I have lived long enough and prayed long enough to know its power. My prayer is not superstition. I do not bargain with God in the manner of "If you do this, I promise that I will...." But I believe that I have an obligation to recognize, thank, and honestly relate to my Maker. I cannot make you do the same. But I do know that, like that athlete who would

win, prayer is worth every hour I have spent doing it.

Start small — perhaps 15 minutes at the beginning or the end of the day, depending on your inner clock. Turn off the phone and the computer, settle in a comfortable chair, and give these moments to God. Don't dwell on all that has been negative this day but hand it over to God to be washed by his love. Do give thanks for what was good — there must have been something, even if it is that a disastrous day has finally ended! — and then take time to reflect. Choose a paragraph or two of a book, a psalm you especially feel drawn to, or a prayer source that is dear to you.

Most of you might choose to do this at night, but I do know people who actually get up a little earlier so that they might begin their day by being centered in this way. You won't be the only one!

Little by little, you might find yourself making a collection of materials for this meditation time: a poem you would like to ponder longer, a book that attracts you, even a passage of scripture. (We will look at the Bible as a source a little later on in greater depth.) The resources are almost infinite.

If we believe the medical professionals, prayer also does something for our bodily health, especially for those of us addicted to multitasking! Meditation calms the mind, lowers blood pressure, stabilizes heartbeat. Prayer is good for body and soul.

Prayer is an exercise, meaning that we have to keep at it. We can't do it twice and then give up. But deliberately woven into our lives, it will become the high point of a day. To be assiduous at the gym or the yoga class is a good thing. To be equally committed to prayer time is even better. It ranks on the top of my self-care list.

When I find myself up against it, as I inevitably do, what do I do? I pray for the grace to find a way to get beyond.

The gift of grace

"Grace" is another of those mysterious spiritual words that many of us don't quite know how to define. Looking at its etymology, we find that it comes from the Latin for "free" or "freely given."

Grace is what happens in those wonderful little moments when an impulse or a thought comes from nowhere like light in a dark place. Or we discover that we have done the seemingly impossible. How? Grace. A solution to the insoluble arrives and — it

27

was grace. The unkind word is not said, I drop the argument that threatens to escalate, I end my "pity party" — how does that happen? Grace.

We live in a grace-strewn, grace-filled world, and we so often miss the meaning of the moment. Years later, however, we might remember to call it grace.

The Bible is filled with examples of such moments, but one of my favorites focuses on Levi, the tax collector. He intrigues me because, by name, he belongs to the tribe of Israel entrusted with Temple worship. When we meet him in the Gospels, he is collecting taxes as an employee of enemy Rome in Capernaum, more than 90 miles from the Temple. It appears that he has somehow failed his family and is in exile. I see him as another prodigal son who has gone astray.

In his need, he has taken a job no self-respecting Jew would have. He is thus further alienated from his own people. I cannot believe he is thrilled with his employment. And then Jesus walks by. It is a moment of grace.

Their eyes meet as Jesus says, "Follow me." Levi leaps up from that bench in his tax collector's booth and he follows. I know he is delighted because he promptly throws a party to celebrate his new life, a life that offers no glamour and no job security, but lifts him from his emotional exile.

It could all have been different. Levi could have shuffled his pile of receipts and thought them more important. He could have mused, "Did I hear him correctly?" He might have procrastinated: "Tomorrow will be a better day to start something new."

He does none of these. He latches on to the grace of the moment before it is lost. His great adventure as an apostle is just beginning.

This grace of the moment is not the only kind of grace. Grace might come after much prayer and thought. It might be the result of faithfully finishing a task just something new beckons.

Grace is everywhere. Once we begin to be more thoughtful about the spiritual journey, we also become more conscious of the fact that we are not doing this alone. We find a strength that might surprise. Having tasted it, we want more, and so prayers for light, assistance or gratitude become more intermingled with the day's activities. Everything is different.

I am not suggesting that prayer is always easy. There are times of the year — Advent, Christmas, Lent — when the very season in our churches seems to invite us to pray. But what about all those other weeks? Many of our church calendars refer to this as "ordinary" time, and that does sound dull! Can we liven it up?

Caring for our hungry souls

Not every day can be a party day. Those "special" times are special because they are so different from our regular routines. We need to look at Ordinary Time with this lens. It allows us to settle into a rhythm where we can pursue a theme or an idea for several days without being interrupted by the need to celebrate something special. It lies closest to what we live in daily life. This lets us tie together our spiritual journey and the demands of every day.

A way to begin is to pray into the very ordinariness of what the day ahead appears to offer. Ask God to be with you as you head to the supermarket, the soccer field, the workplace. Each of those places automatically acquires an aura as it becomes not just a part of the routine but an adventure where you and God are traveling together.

Ordinary Time can also be the period when you read a page or two of that spiritual book you have long wanted to explore, or some bit of the Bible that seemed intriguing. Here is where a little spiritual backpack of ideas for the less celebratory days of the year can be so useful.

And don't forget the prayers that you know by heart, like the "Our Father" or "The Lord Is My Shepherd" or the words of a favorite hymn. Take them phrase by phrase, quietly and reflectively, so that you know why they are in your mind.

Ever so gradually, we begin to realize that we are so much more than the physical body we present to the public. The efforts to cultivate our inner longings for something deeper give meaning to the mundane in our lives. So little in our culture feeds this part of us. We must take care of our hungry souls.

~3~

"IS THERE A GOD? SOMETIMES THIS VERY IDEA SEEMS SO DISTANT FROM MY LIFE OF COMPUTERS AND LAUNDRY AND THE SUPERMARKET. IS HE REAL? DOES CHURCH FIT IN ANYWHERE?"

IS THERE A GOD? If I say "yes" and you say "no," we are at an impasse. I do not believe we can *prove* much about God, but I do believe there is much we can *know*. What do I mean?

Our earliest human ancestors left records on cave walls and through their artifacts of attempts to wrestle with the idea of forces they could not control but which were real. Religion of some sort has been part of the human psyche since the dawn of history. Atheism is a rather late human view, gathering strength at the end of the 19th century — but more about that later.

The fact that God doesn't fit neatly into a proof category should not disqualify him from our conversation. There are other great "unprovables" in our lives: love, hope, courage. We recognize them when we see them in action, but they are hard to "prove" to someone who has never known them.

For example, I think back to a student I taught years ago who had been emotionally abused by parents who neither wanted nor loved her. There was no way she could respond to anything I tried to teach about human love in literature or a loving God in life.

Many years later, she met a wonderful man who loved her and who affirmed the goodness she had never recognized in herself. Then and only then could she begin to know a God of love.

The concept of God suddenly looms large for some people when disaster strikes. Someone has to be blamed and then God becomes useful. It is wise to think about God before you reach this point.

There are so many concepts that boggle my mind from the laws of geometry to the stars in the sky. (As tiny children, we were on to something when we recited "Twinkle, twinkle, little star; how I wonder what you are...") While I do marvel at man's ingenuity in sending Rovers to traverse the Martian terrain, I marvel even more at the very existence of Mars, just seemingly waiting all these eons for someone to find a way to let eyes see its stark beauty.

Scientific discoveries do just what that word says. They uncover something that exists. Where did Mars come from? What is electricity? I deeply respect what science and human intelligence have given us, but I keep wondering who made the mind of man.

Faith, for me, is a trusting beyond proofs, an excitement that we humans of any era do not have all the answers. There is the unspoken promise that there is more to know. This is the stimulus that makes the human journey so intriguing and so much a reason not to close the book on life.

Most of us have laughed at the naïveté of the head of the U.S. Patent Office who petitioned for the closing of his office at the end of the 19th century since all possible new inventions had already been made! Some would relegate God to a drawer in that office, but let's probe a bit.

Where is there a place for God?

Those of us who have a faith tradition rooted in Judeo-Christianity are the heirs of a fascinating clash of ideas. Imagine a Jew entering the Greco-Roman world, and finding himself in foreign intellectual territory. The Greek pantheon of deities embodies all the loves, lusts, trickeries, and hatreds that are found among people everywhere. The deities are indeed made in the image of man.

The Jew has a different theology. His biblical God has made human beings in the divine image. He is good and wants the good even when the human creature has difficulty measuring up. This gives a "God language" that many of us still use.

The great pieces of Greek literature center around a human being struggling against fate and deities pitted against him for often capricious reasons. The key moments in the Hebrew Bible also highlight man's striving for the good but often missing the mark. But in the Bible, the possibility of starting again, of needing and receiving forgiveness becomes a key component.

Unfortunately, we do not always follow through with these ideas in our daily living. In dark times, God gets blamed. In good times, God is pushed into the background as unnecessary. Does that sound familiar?

Make yourself known to God before you have a problem. Then you will not come to him as a stranger in times of need. Our sense of self is closely linked to our ideas of God. If I see myself as the center of the world, if I worship my accomplishments and expect others to do the same, where is there a place for God? Even without a label, I am then a practical atheist.

Since church as institution is no longer either the neighborhood anchor or the prime place for social interaction, atheism has become more common. Because its most public proponents are scientists and men of intellect like Richard Dawkins, Sam Harris, and Daniel Dennett, atheism has also achieved a certain cachet among intellectuals or those who would like to so categorize themselves that way.

I would like to interject here that people of faith are often accused of being afraid to think and of taking refuge in faith as a virtuous substitute for doing real mental work. (I have been accused of both, and worse!) If one's faith is a kind of pie-in-the-sky, all-will-be-made-right-in-heaven belief, then perhaps there is justice in the accusation. But let's assume a robust faith, a vigorous search for truth, and a genuine conviction that God does exist — then I have the right to respond to some of the atheists' arguments.

I said respond, not debate. Religious debates are futile pittings of two sets of convictions against each other. No one, in the end, sees truth in the other's position.

And I might be an atheist, too, if the god I was denying is the one that atheist Richard Dawkins sarcastically calls "the Old Testament's psychotic delinquent." He blithely assembles a list of anthropomorphic images of God from a variety of Old Testament books and emerges with this weird being. Since Dawkins also airily says Christianity was founded by Paul of Tarsus, it becomes a futile task to cite all the instances where he and the believer differ.

It is too easy to take quotations out of context, as many atheists do with the Bible and as we believers often do with the writings of the atheists. I will respect anyone's sincere search for truth. Mockery is not an honest tool in religious discussion.

Dawkins extends his disdain to the agnostics, that other category of the non-religious, who are not sure they can know about the realm of the supernatural. They are on the lookout for evidence, evidence that Dawkins with his irony and Sam Harris with his deeper anger feel has long been available. Therefore, say the atheists, get off the fence and join us. As Dawkins puts it, "Either God exists or he doesn't. It is a scientific question."

To that I have to say, "No, it is a scientific question only to the scientists." The poet, the theologian, and the humanist would all beg to differ. Not everything has an answer in modern science.

The ire of the atheists is further fueled by the current religio-political discussion about whether the United States was founded as a Christian nation. The evidence seems fairly clear that it was not. Among the Founding Fathers there were Christians, but the majority of them were Deists, a widespread 18th-century response to the Enlightenment. The Deist believes in a supernatural intelligence whose activities are confined to setting up the laws that govern the universe. This being is often explained by the example of the clockmaker who sets his work in motion and leaves it on its own after that.

We know that Thomas Jefferson excised all the miracles from his version of the New Testament. And we also know that Benjamin Franklin has been said to have been more interested in the fire wagons of Philadelphia than in the eternal fires of hell!

It seems fair to say that in the Colonial world, where the memories of religious persecution were strong, it would have been unthinkable to set up a Christian nation politically, whatever the personal beliefs of individual Founding Fathers. However, they were not atheists by any modern twisting of that word.

This discussion naturally flows into an adjoining modern category, the "spiritual but not religious" category. Its adherents often explain that being religious means holding on to senseless rules and regulations from churches with hidebound dogmas. They want to be free to be more broad-minded and intelligent about their path to the spiritual.

These are not fanatics — they exist among believers and disbelievers alike — nor are they the ones who equate faith with irrationality. The "sincerely spiritual but not religious" are often on long journeys to satisfy their deep needs. It is here that the lure of the East, with practices of chant, meditation, and silence, is most appealing in our noisy urban Western world. The Asian guru can seem to speak with greater wisdom than a spiritual director from one's own milieu.

However, we need to be cautious of adopting practices from cultures not our own. If we want them to bear lasting fruit where we are rooted, we must make sure that we understand the cultural mores in which they are rooted.

There is always the temptation to make our spirituality all about ourselves. We are all egoists at heart. A healthy spiritual journey should help us see that there are others in our orbit, others with something to give us and with needs that we might be called to meet. A spirituality focused totally on self is ultimately diminishing.

Some New Age practitioners of self-obsession and aversion to authority found those beliefs taking root during the Vietnam War protests of the 1960s. That hippie, free-love, "take to the road" world still has its echoes today. Why?

One answer is easy: We each find our selves to be so interesting! That same self is less intriguing to a neighbor equally preoccupied with himself. What is shared is a desire to step aside into a world without boundaries where the individual rules.

I remember a former student from the 1960s who renounced a laboriously prepared-for career in education for a new life in a commune. She gave her children names reminiscent of the period, and there was not an antiwar march in which she and her partner did not participate. Years later, I had one of her sons as a student. She came to a PTA meeting to lament the fact that she had picked up his notebook and found it filled with drawings of guns.

"Why?" she cried. "I am so against war in every form."

I asked, "Did it ever occur to you that he, in his adolescent rebelliousness, has to be against your principles just as you were against those of your parents?"

She looked at me aghast. Still dressed in hippie fashion, still looking for a cause to protest, she was horrified that her child could not be of the same mind. He, by the way, went on to become a member of the middle class: traditionally employed, married, and with his own children. I have often wondered how he explains this grandmother to the next generation.

Another characteristic of the New Age is to sample everything, to taste the religious offerings of many denominations, but to commit to none of them. We have all met the parents who religiously (ah!) take their offspring from church to temple to synagogue on weekends so that the youngsters might make a permanent choice of their own. Such open-mindedness can lead to a mind with no sides at all.

The dictionary defines the spiritual as "relating to the mind, will, and feeling part of a human being," while religion is "belief in a supernatural power" with the added proviso that religion is usually an "institutionalized system grounded in such belief."

Thus the question arises of church versus a more freewheeling spirituality tailored to me alone. Surely, as my high school students used to say, "I can pray just as well at home." And I would respond, "And do you?" That is the rub.

Stepping outside of self

I know that for me to truly slake my soul's thirst, I need two sources for my spiritual journey. First, I need to create time and quiet for my own conversing with God, for owning my needs and frailties, and for being more open to others.

I also need the challenge that comes from being with others, sharing their joys and pains, adding my prayers to theirs, and stepping outside myself long enough to acknowledge that I do not walk this planet Earth alone.

So, when asked the question, can one "do" religion on one's own, the answer is both yes and no. I do not wear rose-colored glasses. I am aware of the fact that every church has a human component that is both strength and weakness. We must not let either the idiosyncrasies or the attractiveness of church leaders become the driving force. Never can we lose sight of our most priceless inner gift, our free will. It belongs to no church or churchman. Robots are not healthy congregants!

At its best, church allows men and women to come together in community to acknowledge their own fallibility, to share joys and sorrows greater than one heart can hold, and to find others with whom they can wrestle with life's challenges as they sit in the presence of a Power greater than any other.

These are simple phrases, but they underlie the shared faith that results in "church." In most cases, it is not doctrine that attracts one to a church group. It is the welcome one receives from a community of like-minded pilgrims. For that reason, I think religion's greatest power lies in the joyous conviction of its proponents.

One of my favorite exercises is to walk past a church on a Sunday and observe the faces of the exiting congregation. If they emerge with smiles, I believe that congregation is doing something right. If they are frowning or glum, something has definitely gone wrong, either in society or in that church. So the group deserves a second or a third visit to see if their faces might change. If they don't, I worry about that community of believers.

In summary, I am convinced that church helps the spiritual journey, but it cannot do the work alone. Most of us go to church one day a week. What we are about on the other six days tests our belief in God and our seriousness about our faith journey.

~4~

"I FEEL GUILTY SINCE I SO OFTEN HAVE QUESTIONS ABOUT BELIEVING. DO THESE DOUBTS MAKE ME BAD?"

IF YOU NEVER HAD QUESTIONS about your faith, I'd be really worried. One of the signs that we are thinking people is our ability to say "Why?" or "How do you know?" The verbal 2-year-old is filled with "whys," and that signals to his or her adoring parents that there is a mind beginning to function. Why should it be different for an adult in matters of faith?

No one has put this better than Abraham Joshua Heschel, a giant of 20th-century Judaism. He says:

> We must never cease to question our faith and to ask what God means to us. Is He an alibi for ignorance? Is He a pretext for comfort and unwarranted cheer?

Heschel goes on to distinguish between faith, the act of believing, and creed, that which we believe. Stop here a moment. That is a vital distinction.

All our life long, we will go on practicing faith on some level, because we cannot live in a state of pure doubt. That would be paralyzing. One of our problems is language. I love the fact that the Hebrew word for faith, *emunah*, is a verb, not a noun. The implication of action rouses us from seeing faith as related to inertia.

We encounter astonishing things every day that we do not fully fathom, but which we do not disbelieve. We wonder as unmanned cameras send back photos from space. We mentally grapple as the media attempt to explain the Higgs boson particle and its significance. We shake our heads as we stand in a museum before a skeletal dinosaur, but we believe the scientists who tell us it actually walked our earth.

In each instance, we exercise human faith that objects not in our realm of experience do exist. Why then should we have such trouble before the tenets of a faith we cannot fully comprehend?

In some instances, it is because we have been taught not to question in all matters religious. In other instances, it is because varying interpretations have become more authoritative than the creeds themselves. In the spirit that Heschel suggests, we must become questioners if we are to weave truth into our lives.

To ask where a teaching comes from and if it is related to culture or custom is to be a thinking person. It is a denial of the gift of God to speak proudly of "blind faith." We are rational beings, and we do not give away that faculty as we come to God.

Rabbi Heschel challenges: "Faith without reason is mute; reason without faith is deaf."

And who was the wise man who said, "I would not believe in a God I could fully understand"? It is an oxymoron, isn't it, to insist that we proud humans can stuff an infinite being into our human minds.

So often, we believers are accused of substituting faith for thought. Not true! Faith is actually an act of humility, an acknowledgment of the possibility that I might not know everything, but that I can know something.

I love the fact that scientists are constantly discovering new realities. Do note — they are not creating. They are discovering, which says to me that they have not yet exhausted all there is to know in any of their given fields. Beyond lie further truths towards which they strive. In the realm of faith, we operate in a similar way.

Those of us who come from the Judeo-Christian tradition have a gift from our ancestors. We will be discussing the Bible at greater length elsewhere, but let's take a minute to look at the unique Hebrew God.

From the dawn of recorded history, mankind has believed there are forces greater than the human. Stone or wooden representations of these deities were an effort to express this reality beyond the human situation.

The Hebrews offer a different perspective from the ones that came before. Their God wants to be a part of their everyday living. He speaks to them, a definite sign of life. Chapter 19 of Exodus records this important turning point in their perception of God. From then on, God, represented by his word on stone tablets, journeys with his people across the desert of Sinai, taking up residence in a tent, just as the tribal members do.

The Hebrews of the Old Testament are never afraid to speak of their God as listening to them and sharing in what they do. This leads to the rather odd image of a God who goes to war with them, who sets up a covenant relationship as if he is another equal human partner, who cares about them. All this is written using the language and customs of a tribal, treaty-making society.

While we might smile at the naïveté of this Iron Age people, there is no denying the reality of this God they cannot see. They know that ultimately the graven images of Moab and Babylon have no power, nor any care for their worshippers. Their living God has both.

They are never afraid to ask questions. Some of the psalms are almost breathtaking in their daring as they verbally shake a fist at a God whom the writers do not always comprehend but whose reality they never doubt.

Before you object that they were really a rather unsophisticated group and we are a technological, scientific people, we need to add a further thought. To question is not to reject. To question is to want to understand. To ask "why" is to dig deeper into the meaning of our lives.

Being whole and being holy

What we believe has to spill over into the fabric of our daily living. It is far too easy to confuse doing good with being good. I'd like to think that most of us want to be decent people. Jesus offers us this challenge in the Sermon on the Mount when he says, "Be perfect, therefore, as your heavenly Father is perfect" (Matt. 5:48). Don't let that scare you. The Greek text is suggesting that we become "whole," as complete as we possibly can become. That is a goal towards which we can reasonably aspire.

To be "whole" is also to be "holy," which is our destiny. Paul loved to refer to members of his first communities as "saints," not because they were, but because they were works in progress.

This is also a goal that fits within our questioning mode. It is human to ask questions of both ourselves and of our God. As we look at the broad religious spectrum, there is so much room for the interrogative mode. We have to work on distinguishing the articles of faith of our denomination from the interpretations that flow from them, as we noted earlier. Do not be afraid to question the difference. If we fail to question, the human interpretations can assume an unbalanced importance and even edge their way into the core beliefs. All this underlines the fact that we never cease being human, even as our souls so often long for more. We recognize this dilemma as we struggle with the priorities of each new day.

Here is where we can draw encouragement from looking at the external circumstances of the life of Jesus. He never withdraws from daily living for any prolonged period of time. He catches early-morning prayer time before stepping back on the road that leads from village to village where he has to teach. He goes at night to find a mountaintop moment of solitude and peace. He refuels, as it were, and finds spiritual energy for a new day.

It is often easy to meet God when we are alone, or on a retreat in some quietly beautiful part of nature. It is harder in the office, the subway, or the marketplace. I say harder. I do not say impossible.

If we are called to be holy where we are, then we are called to be everyday mystics. The word "mystics" is scarier than the idea of holiness since it conjures up visions of heavenly voices. It shouldn't. What it should do is remind us of the reality of God in our lives.

As we rush along from place to place, we try to remember that God is coming along with us. This consciousness, even if it only penetrates once or twice a day, is a God-thought that changes us.

I love the practice of a young man I met in one of my lunchtime groups. He told us that he had glued a card to his door, next to the lock that he had to undo in order to leave the apartment. It read, "This day is yours, God. Help me to use it for you."

He noted, "I often forget during the day. But each morning I renew my commitment and that makes everything different."

In my book, he is a mystic.

We each need to find a way to trigger similar moments in our everyday lives. The modern mystic has a family with very real needs for dinner and soccer practice and clean laundry. The modern mystic has a never-ending "to do" list, but is also aware that whatever he or she does is part of holy living this day. This is just as true a calling from God as a message received by a desert hermit of the 4th century.

Those early Christians referred to as "saints" were as prone to slipping as any of us, but they knew they had a greater destiny. We need to remind ourselves of this again and again.

The modern holy one might not be bathed in a stained-glass glow but is rather chairing a meeting. The modern holy one carpools and grocery shops and is walking next to me on the sidewalk. The modern holy one offers a hand to the next-door neighbor and a smile to the store clerk. The modern holy one knows that both speech and silence come from within and weighs the time for each. The modern holy one loves laughter and prayer because they are both so essentially human and so God-given.

Our call to holiness is not scary but is part of our very being. Is it stirring within?

~5~

"WHERE MIGHT I GO TO FIND WHAT OTHERS HAVE LEARNED ABOUT THIS SPIRITUAL JOURNEY? IS THERE A BOOK THAT MIGHT HELP?"

MANY WISE MEN AND WOMEN have written about their spiritual journeys, and their experiences can make for helpful reading. However, I'd like to make a plea that you start with the best-selling book of all time, the Bible.

I have no idea what your previous encounters with the Bible have been like, nor do I have a clue as to what you already know, or think you know. But there is no way we can dismiss this source in which the three great monotheistic religions — Judaism, Christianity, and Islam — all find common ancestors. It has to be considered.

My own experience might be relevant. I grew up in a religious but not Bible-based family. We did not even own a Bible. I knew some biblical stories from school lessons, and I was conversant with Jesus and the Gospels, but I was really pretty ignorant of most of scripture. By an unexpected set of circumstances, I found myself in Rome at a graduate school of theology and, of course, the Bible was part of the curriculum.

My mind was virgin territory. I was 25 years old, and I was just about as biblically ignorant as one could be. But the light bulb went on for me the day I was working on a text in Jeremiah, a passage in which the prophet felt called to change his life in order to warn his people of great danger ahead. He decided he would not marry nor attend the festive celebrations of his fellow citizens in Jerusalem. When they would inevitably ask "Why?" he would tell them that they were dancing on the edge of an abyss. The invading armies of Babylon were just over the horizon, and disaster was coming. They needed to lift their heads from the sand and prepare for the worst.

As I worked through the text, it struck me like a thunderbolt that Jeremiah was a flesh-and-blood human being living in a dreadful moment of history. His words were being tossed back in his face by his heedless fellow citizens. How alienated and alone he much have felt. I was overwhelmed by what he was going through. For a moment, he was so real that I was sure that if I lifted my eyes from the page, he would be sitting across the library table from me. I was too petrified to move.

Happily, that moment passed. I looked up and there was no one else at that table but me, thank God. However, what happened there changed everything in my approach to the biblical texts from then on. I made a kind of private vow that if circumstances ever let me teach others about the Bible, I would emphasize the humanity of those involved, rather than any one doctrine. It is an entryway into a great text.

I often want to weep as I pass street corner preachers or listen to some of the Christian "experts" expounding on TV. Their blind literalism and depiction of the Bible as an answer book for every one of life's ills would never have moved an Abraham or a Moses.

I do realize that Jeremiah might look a bit strange in Starbucks today, but so would George Washington. History determined when they lived and how they moved through life. But history does not make them meaningless to us.

That is the first point I would like to make about the Bible in general. It deals with real people who have real problems, just like you and me. You might ask here, "So what? I have my own issues, thank you very much."

Indeed you do. However, the enormous popularity of advice columns and talk-show catharsis moments is rooted in the human need to know what others think we should or could do next. Can anything be learned from those who have lived before us? If it can't, are we forever condemned to reinventing the wheel?

Reading the Bible is not just a kind of spiritual archeology but an eye-opening discovery of the spiritual origins of a monotheistic people, convinced that their God communicated with them. We find their record of what was shared around campfires and carried in their memories as they moved across the Mideast. At a time when all those around them had multiple deities of stone or wood, the Hebrews clung to the word of a single God who had made it clear that religion was not only ceremony and ritual, but a model code that required consideration for other people.

Those of us in the Western world wrestle with the Bible's ideas in our politics and in our cultural heritage. I recall a conversation I had with a professor at a large French university. The school had had to create a new position in religious history because the art history students were no longer able to understand the subject matter of the master works they were studying. The young unchurched do not know what is meant by "The Adoration of the Magi" or "David Ravishing Bathsheba." Who are these people from the Bible?

Religious literacy is so low that great art has become incomprehensible. I know this isn't the best reason for knowing the Bible, but it is one that previous generations might have taken for granted. The Bible is actually hanging, scene by scene, in our major museums.

Why else should you know something about the Bible? For the sheer humanity of the characters. I have often jokingly said that if I were to be marooned on a desert island, I would like to have two books with me: an unabridged dictionary and a Bible. (I do realize I'll have trouble getting the first into my lifeboat!) However, with them, I could recreate civilization, have great discussions with my fellow "maroonees," and be entertained for the years until we are rescued. Genesis alone includes the plots of every soap opera imaginable!

It is to me enormously encouraging that the people who stream across the pages of the Bible are as much a mixture of good and less good as those I encounter in daily living. In other words, they are real.

I might also add that in a world where travelers knock themselves out to have exotic experiences in far-flung places, they might also consider a trek into the world of the Bible. For some, it might be stranger than Nepal or the ocean's depths. It also requires much less packing!

Are you beginning to see why I think the Bible is such a rich quarry?

The Bible as library

Let's pick up this library and see what we might find. It's important to remember that the Bible is not really a book, but a collection of books by different human authors and from different periods of history. For that reason, let's think of it as a library.

As with any library, there are books of many types: legends, history, fiction, poetry, short stories, songs, political commentary, census results, and beyond. If you can name a genre, the Bible probably has a sample of it.

As you turn the first pages of the Bible, do not be put off as you read "Old Testament," which is the Christian name for the Hebrew Bible. "Old" in this case does not mean outdated. It is better translated as "first." If we are at all serious about better understanding the Bible, we have to start here and interact with these people.

To miss this part of the Bible would be to miss knowing one of the more remarkable groups of people who have walked our earth. It is true that these Hebrews built no lasting monuments, explored no unknown lands, nor did they invent anything as revolutionary as the wheel or the sailing vessel. They did more.

They have shared with us their cherished belief in a God who made, by his word, all that crosses the heavens, all that lives on our earth, and all that is found beneath the seas. And creation is crowned by this revolutionary statement: "So God created humankind in his image, in the image of God he created them; male and female he created them" (Gen. 1:27).

If this image is not physical, then where do we find the God-likeness in human beings? It has to be within: in our ability to understand the world, to make choices, and to be responsible for them. It is the very gift we are exercising at this moment, as we confront a text and ask ourselves what these words might mean, both literally and in their implications. No other creature can do that.

The most useful rule I have learned for reading the Bible comes from the scholar

Dianne Bergant, who asks: What did it mean then? What does it mean now? And what are we to do with it? These three steps can keep us from fanciful wanderings and can make the Bible a more useful tool on the journey.

This is also a warning about that often-heard phrase, "The Bible says..." It is so easy and so wrong to start a discussion that way. No, the *Bible* doesn't say anything. A book of the Bible says things. Each book of this library is set in an approximate era. Tribal life in the polygamous Iron Age of Jacob and family life in the Greco-Roman world of Paul are separated by centuries.

In summary, we know the Bible does not ask to be read literally. Instead, it challenges us to seek the same great truths that our biblical ancestors sought. Is there a God? Is there a moral code that makes us humans different from the animals? What role do our own choices play in our fate? Since life involves a journey we share with others, what does that require of us?

"I THOUGHT A SPIRITUAL JOURNEY INVOLVED EMOTIONS AND FEELINGS. YOU SEEM TO BE SUGGESTING THAT I WRESTLE WITH WORDS AND IDEAS. HAVE I MISUNDERSTOOD?"

NO — YOU'RE RIGHT ON TARGET! The biggest mistake people can make when they begin a faith journey is to think that feelings are of prime importance. I am really trying to set you up for the long haul, for those bleak days when you might feel that God has disappeared and you haven't a hope of finding a spiritual thought.

Long-time believers have a name for this — spiritual dryness — but we won't worry about that. Let's simply say that there will be days when you don't feel like it. Since so much of what we do depends on what we feel, it is only natural to want to give up at times like this.

I am suggesting that being serious about the spiritual life is comparable to being serious about exercise or anything else that fits into the concept of routine. Regardless of how you feel, you have to do it so that you don't lose the ground you have already gained.

The excitement of being serious about a text in the Bible is in applying those three rules from the last chapter. Put yourself in the picture and ask about the world behind the text. Life in a tribal Middle Eastern society is not quite like life in 21st-century America. Then look for the deeper truth. Despite the differences in customs and culture, is anything happening in the text that has meaning for you? Do the words resonate with your current situation? If you could, what advice might you give the person in the text? What might he or she say to you?

These are the techniques that make literature come alive. But when the Bible is in question, we too often say that it isn't just literature. It is the Word of God and I cannot question it. Wrong! Any masterwork has to be unlayered, read and reread, argued with and digested. An example from my years as an English teacher might help here.

I once had a grant to study *Hamlet* in a group of 15. We read intensely, parsed the lines, and viewed various versions of the text filmed across the years. At the end of our month together, we all realized that our intense labors had only proved to us that a masterwork needs more than 30 days. It needs a lifetime!

Something very similar can be said of the Bible. To this day, I find something new every time I open its pages, not because I haven't seen those words before but because I am today someone I was not last month or last year.

That is the effect of literature that is timeless. We've only had the Bible for three millennia, so we have much still to discover!

Any skill requires practice and more practice. Athletes are the most obvious example of this, but we can all subscribe to the adage, "Use it or lose it."

If you come from a church background that discouraged this kind of active reading of the Bible, you might have to do a bit of violence to your earlier ideas. I have a student in an adult Bible class who had been taught an extremely conservative, literal approach to the Bible. The ability to ask questions and to put new meanings into outdated words has been like a light in a dark place to him. He says, "I come to this class to get my brain rewired."

I am delighted that he cares enough to undertake that spiritual renovation. If you have ever worked at remodeling an old house, there might be times when it will seem easier to tear the whole thing down and start over. Don't give up. Whether you come from plenty or paucity, you will discover there is absolutely nothing that equals the thrill of having a scripture passage come alive for you.

Another trick I have learned through time is that something happens when more than one sense is involved. Instead of reading the words silently, try reading them aloud. So often an idea is more vivid when it is heard as well as seen.

Jewish Christians

There does remain that further large question about the Bible. Is it Jewish or Christian or — ? As some of those old religious walls that used to divide us are disappearing, we have to look more closely at our roots. And inevitably the question will arise as to how Jesus fits into Judaism.

The Jewish Jesus

The Jewish Jesus is a concept we cannot avoid. Quite simply, Jesus was born a Jew, lived as a faithful and observant one his entire life, and died and was buried as one. Given the wide variety of expressions of Judaism in the first-century world, there was a place for him.

Jesus was not a Christian, heretical as this might seem. Nowhere does any Gospel depict his message in any light except as part of a growing, expanding message totally rooted in Judaism.

It is interesting to study this idea at Jesus' final instructional moment, the Last Supper. He is gathered with his closest followers for a Passover meal. The brief records of what he said and did at that meal focus a light on his Jewishness.

First, look for a moment at what he does. On a table that holds a roasted lamb and dishes of other foods, there is also bread, the most basic food of every Mediterranean and Near Eastern meal, and a cup of watered wine, the daily beverage of all. Jesus passes these elements and gives them new meaning.

Whatever your theology of the Communion elements, far too complex for consideration here, certain things are common to all Christian believers. Jesus ignores the sacrificial lamb of this festival, and instead gives new meaning to the simplest of foods. There would never be a meal without bread and wine. Even in our own context, these elements are essential to many dinner tables. Therefore, the universal reminder of his ongoing presence is powerfully symbolized.

Then look at the words as recorded in Matthew's Gospel, the most Jewish of the four evangelists. Jesus speaks of the cup as the new symbol of the covenant, which is to be expressed in terms of forgiveness.

There are too many people who think of forgiveness as something specifically Christian. It is not. It is thoroughly embedded in the Old Testament. One of the most beautiful examples is found as early as the book of Genesis in the Joseph saga that begins in Chapter 37 and spirals on through Chapter 50.

Very briefly, Joseph is sold into slavery by his brothers and finds himself in Egypt. In a time of disaster, he rises to heights of governance and administers the grain silos of the Pharaoh during years of famine.

His brothers arrive to buy grain and fail to recognize the now adult Joseph, so different from the adolescent they had betrayed. After a few tricks, Joseph reveals who he is to his terrified siblings who fear his wrath. Instead, he says that God has brought good out of evil. Joseph arranges to move the entire family into Egypt, including his aged father, Jacob, and continues to provide for them. After Jacob dies, the brothers, still distrustful of Joseph because they distrust themselves, concoct a story that the last thing Jacob said on his deathbed was that they were to be forgiven. Joseph knows they fear his revenge. He simply says, "Do not be afraid! Am I in the place of God?" There is no retaliation.

This need for forgiveness is as old as these primitive Bible stories. Jesus is so aware of this as at this final meal he begs his disciples to remember that sharing food is also sharing that gift of God which we can give each other, forgiveness. The disciples are going to need this before this night is over. One of them will become a betrayer; one will deny he ever heard of Jesus; all will flee. Before another meal can be shared, much will need forgiving.

John's Gospel also links the concept of forgiveness to his Easter message. First, in a garden on that Sunday morning, Jesus' friend Mary Magdalene is given words to take to the frightened disciples. The resurrected Jesus tells her, "Go to my brothers and say to them, 'I am ascending to my Father and your Father, to my God and your God.'"

If that isn't clear enough that the disciples are still in the "family" despite their failures, Jesus himself will come to them in the evening to wish them "Shalom" and then to say, "Receive the Holy Spirit. If you forgive the sins of any, they are forgiven them; if you retain the sins of any, they are retained" (John 20:23). To be unable to forgive even yourself is to be paralyzed and frozen in place. These disciples have to be free to move forward.

Given the wide variety in first-century Judaism, there was no need for the followers of Jesus to think of themselves as in any way separate from other Jews. Just as some of their contemporaries were followers of the rabbis Hillel or Shammai, they belonged to Jesus of Nazareth.

But change was coming. On the fringes of Judaism across the Roman world stood groups of Gentiles, pagans who respected the moral code of Judaism. Surrounded by the multiplicity of Roman deities, they longed for the single, moral God of their Jewish neighbors. They were referred to as "God-fearers" and were allowed to attend synagogue services and to enter the court-yard of the Temple, but not the inner areas.

We know from archeological evidence that many of these "God-fearers" contrib-uted to the building of synagogues and were held in esteem by Jews, even as they re-mained outside the family circle. Most first-century Jews felt that one had to be born into Mosaic law in order to fulfill it.

The first of these sympathetic pagans to knock on the Jewish-Christian door after Je-sus had left this earth is an unnamed Ethio-pian eunuch from the court of the queen of that country. He is on the Gaza Road, heading home, as he reads from a scroll of Isaiah that he purchased in Jerusalem. The evangelist Philip draws near to his chariot and the eunuch asks him to explain the text.

After what must have been an enlighten-ing lesson, the eunuch asks for baptism, and so becomes the first known Gentile to join the Jesus group. This could have passed un-noticed by the religious authorities since his chariot goes on to Ethiopia and he is heard from no more (Acts 8:26-40).

The second such request is much more public. It comes from Cornelius, a Roman centurion stationed in Caesarea, who asks for baptism for himself and his household. His plea is addressed to Peter, who journeys north from Joppa to meet this group. He is in admiration at the sincerity of their request and concludes, "I truly understand that God shows no partiality" (Acts 10:34). Peter's actions cannot pass unnoticed.

Peter is called to headquarters in Jerusalem to give an accounting. (It is interesting that he is not the one in charge.) The hardliners want these pagans to be circumcised and to take on the full demands of the Mosaic Law as a prelude to baptism. Peter demurs, pleading that the Spirit of God was active in them. He argues, "If then God gave to them the same gift that he gave to us when we believed in the Lord Jesus Christ, who was I that I could hinder God?" His hearers are silenced for the moment (Acts 11:17-18).

The rub, as it were, lies in the manner that these followers of Jesus worshiped. On the Sabbath they prayed with their neighbors in the synagogue. On the first day of the week, Jew and Gentile together repeated what Jesus had done on his last night among them. They shared a meal, retold the Jesus story, and prayed for their needs. It was the meal that posed the problem.

In that culture, one did not eat with outsiders and some still considered these Gentiles as strangers. Some Jewish Christians were uneasy to find Gentiles welcomed at the table, something that Paul and his partner Barnabas were openly doing as they preached across the eastern roads of the Roman Empire. The conservatives in Jerusalem demanded a clear answer. In Acts 15, both sides are represented at a gathering in Jerusalem, presided over by James, brother of Jesus. In a lively debate, traditionalists and innovators give their respective viewpoints. Some of the fire is still palpable in the sanitized version that has been recorded.

James listens and then decides in favor of allowing the Gentiles to join the group without first becoming Jews. There are some food restrictions and a moral admonition, but these are minor. Non-Jews can now become followers of Jesus.

Two things would happen within the next few decades that forever changed the relationship between Jews and Jewish Christians. Roman patience with the rebellious Jewish province of Palestine was exhausted by the year 70 A.D. The Roman army destroyed Jerusalem, burning the Temple and looting its contents. This was devastating to Judaism. Never again would the smoke of sacrifice rise from an altar. The priesthood would disappear, its functions now impossible to perform.

For the second time in 600 years, the Jews lost the heart of their religious life. At this time the Pharisees, the official interpreters of the Law, took on a more prominent role. They reminded a grief-ravaged people that God was not lost; he was ever-present in his word, which they still had on their scrolls and in their hearts. The synagogue assembly was the new focus of their life.

As so often happens in a time of crisis, the conservative voices became the dominant ones. The Pharisees focused on the Jewish Christians who still worshipped with them and decided that they must choose. A meeting of Jewish leaders at Jamnia around the year 90 added a mandatory set of prayers to each synagogue service in which a curse was called down on the Christians. Christians could not, in good conscience, say it, and so they finally separated from their neighbors.

We can sense some of the anguish of this time in John's Gospel, with its very strong statements against "the Jews." The author's anger is directed against the Jewish leadership that is forcing this division. Those being made to leave still saw themselves as Jews at heart.

To me, there is nothing more touching in the letters of Paul than chapter 11 of his letter to the Romans. He remains fiercely proud of his Judaism as he speaks of his hopes for those who would forever be his people. He uses the analogy of an olive tree with rich roots, into which a wild olive shoot, the Gentiles, has been grafted. He warns these Gentiles not to boast since it is this root that gives them life. He dreams that one day the natural branch might be grafted back.

I am always near tears as I read these words. Paul so rightly loved the source that had made him who he was. By the call of God, his ministry was to the Gentiles, but he needed to remind them that Judaism was the life-source for their journey. Even today, we Christians cannot forget this.

When our brothers in Islam speak of Abraham, Moses, Jesus, and the prophets, they are delving into the same heritage. These three monotheistic religions were born in the same part of the world and claim this same root, which makes religious quarrels among them so sad. They grow from the same source.

Abraham

No one stands taller in the biblical story than Abraham, revered by Jews as

"the father of those who believe"; by Muslims as "khalil Allah," the "friend of Allah"; and by the Christians as the fore-father of Jesus. No one else is claimed in the same way in the three great mono-theistic religions.

Abraham strides out of the mists of prehistory into Genesis somewhere in the 19th century B.C. He is a monotheist from Ur of the Chaldees (southern Iraq to-day). He comes from a city noted for its worship of Sin, the mood goddess, so there are no clues as to the origins of his faith. However, the first words God ad-dresses to him are the beginning of a long walk along the Fertile Crescent into the Land of Promise. God says, "Go from your country and your kindred and your father's house to the land that I will show you." (Gen. 12:1). This sets in mo-tion centuries of wandering by a no-madic people.

In the midst of this journeying, Abra-ham learns that human sacrifice is not pleasing to his deity; he separates from his nephew, Lot, the last of his family; he meets a mysterious king from Salem who offers a tribute of bread and wine; and he tries, with difficulty, to sire a son so that his name will not vanish from this earth. The begetting of this child gives Muslims their place in the story.

Abraham's wife, Sarah, seems to be barren. Following the customs of the patriarchal world, she gives her Egyptian slave, Hagar, to Abraham, so that a child might carry on the family line. Hagar conceives, setting up a jealous rivalry within the tent. The outsider has succeeded in doing what Sarah could not.

Sarah drives Hagar out into the wilderness where this slave becomes the first woman in the Bible to experience an annunciation (Gen. 16). She is told by an angel to return to Abraham, and is given the name for her unborn son. Back she goes. When the child is born, Abraham claims him with that name. He is Ishmael, a name from the Hebrew root "God has heard."

Years later, when Sarah has finally had her own son, Isaac, Hagar is again driven out with little Ishmael. Once again, God comes to her aid, with the promise that Ishmael too shall become a great nation. God keeps his promise. Ishmael grows up in the wilderness and, after Hagar procures a wife for him from

Egypt, he becomes the father of 12 sons, thus ensuring his posterity.

Genesis also records that, many years later, when Abraham dies, his two sons, Isaac and Ishmael, bury him together (Gen. 25:9). So there seems to have been no permanent estrangement between the sons.

All of this is background for Muhammad's vocation in the seventh century A.D. He worried that the Arabs had been omitted from the divine plan since they did not have a deity, a revelation, or a prophet of their own. Constant tribal warfare further cut them off from the rest of the world. All this changed the day that Muhammad was overpowered by a presence that revealed a new scripture to him, the Koran.

It did not seem to him to be a new religion, but rather a return to the great basic truths of Allah who created the world for which mankind was responsible. Unfortunately, Muhammad's explanation of his call was rejected by both Jews and Christians, whom he tried in vain to convince of his sincerity. Islam gradually became a third monotheistic religion in the Near East.

Muhammad's faith led him to see that Ishmael, too, was a desert tribal man. When he discovered that local tradition said Hagar and Ishmael had settled near Mecca and that Abraham and Ishmael had together rebuilt the cabala, he was ecstatic. Here was a lost son of Abraham waiting to find a place of prominence in the story of God's dealings with humankind.

Muhammad saw his revelation as part of what already existed, and so, for generations, he discouraged conversions. He taught that all people belonged to the People of the Book, be they Jew, Christian, or Muslim, since all descended from the same father, Abraham.

It is useless to speculate on what might have been had he been able to pass on his original ideas of Islam as a non-militaristic religion that gave its women rights neither Judaism nor Christianity had yet embraced. So much was lost with the rise of more militaristic successors of Muhammad, and the bloodshed that still roils the world.

With tragic consequences, we forget Muhammad's original discovery of a place for his people in the divine plan.

This might be a very long answer to your initial question about why we wrestle with the Bible. Have I given you anything more to think about? Are you ready with some new insights to look at the Bible as a possible companion for a spiritual journey?

~7~

"MAYBE I'M A COWARD, BUT I AM REALLY AFRAID TO OPEN THE BIBLE. I AM NOT SURE I WANT TO MEET THE GOD I THINK IS THERE. IS THERE ANY HELP FOR ME?"

DON'T WORRY. Yours is an almost universal problem. Many people grew up in families with that large book that was useful for pressing flowers or for recording family transitions, but that was too formidable to be actually read.

You probably have a dozen questions, and one of them is probably what it means to call this library, the Bible, the "Word of God." An easy way to start a fervid discussion among people of faith is to ask them what they mean by those words.

For some Christians, it means that God dictated every word and idea to human authors who dutifully wrote them down. For others, it means that the concepts in the Bible were inspired by God, but the very human authors put them into words that were meaningful in their time and place. You might want to think about these differing concepts of inspiration.

A second source of puzzlement comes from the fact that many parts of the Bible deal with a world and a culture almost 4,000 years old. It is not our 21st-century milieu, to say the least. We cannot expect the people in it to act as we might, nor are we asked to literally imitate them. Here is where we need our intelligence to guide us.

Some of the indignation at biblical "teachings" comes from a failure to take culture into account. Directives given to members of Iron Age clans cannot be taken word for word in our search for spiritual enlightenment. But the spirit behind such directives does need to be considered.

Thirdly, the writers of the Bible did not speak English, and no part of the Bible was written in our language. We insult the God who gave us our intelligence when we insist on reading a text word for word. The bulk of the Old Testament was written in ancient Hebrew, a language with a fairly limited vocabulary, but one that uses puns and word-play. Translators often have to strain to find English equivalents.

Translations

The Bible was never meant to be foreign to the lives of its readers. For that

reason, it has always needed to be translated and retranslated as languages change.

The Old Testament was originally written in Hebrew, with a few Aramaic passages. They were the languages then in common use. But by the second century B.C., Greek was more widely used. Hence, a Greek version, the Septuagint, was made. Its unusual name, meaning 70, comes from the legend that 70 men were asked to do this work. They went into their separate cubicles and emerged, 70 days later, with 70 identical versions of the Bible! There might be too many 70s in that story, but that Greek translation became the one in common use for centuries.

The entire New Testament was written in Greek, since neither Hebrew nor Aramaic was a common spoken language by then. This enabled the Christian message to spread rapidly in that Greek-speaking Roman world.

By the 4th century A.D., however, Latin had moved from official documents into the language of common use. Jerome, the greatest scholar of his day, was commissioned to translate the Bible into that language. His monumental Latin translation, the Vulgate, became the new standard.

As local languages began to develop in the early Middle Ages, ordinary people no longer had access to the text of the Bible. They relied on church art or on poetic renderings, such as that produced by Caedmon, the first English poet. Little by little, the Bible became the possession of clerics, since the laity could no longer read it. The rumblings of a need for overall reform included a cry for access to the Word of God.

In 1382, John Wycliffe published an English translation of the entire Bible, which was promptly burned by church authorities. But a tide was turning, and his efforts were followed by those of others, all impelled by the invention of the printing press. Since most of these translations were accompanied by explanatory footnotes, church authorities became understandably nervous, since individuals could now decide for themselves what a verse might mean.

In England, this tension came to a climax in 1603, when King James I came to the throne. Distressed by the inaccuracies of some translations and by non-authoritative interpretations, he commissioned a band of scholars to produce an "official" English Bible from the original Hebrew and Greek texts.

It might surprise us to learn that the resulting King James Bible of 1612 was not universally welcomed, because many people thought its language was too modern. (The first edition was almost immediately recalled since a typographical error rendered one of the Ten Commandments as "Thou shalt commit adultery"!)

It would take more than 40 years for this Bible to work its way into widespread acceptance. However, it gradually became the standard text for many Protestant churches. This was due in large measure to the insistence of James that special care be taken to the sound of the language, as this text was destined to be read aloud.

The work of translation will never be finished. As more ancient manuscripts are unearthed, more clues will be offered both to better texts and to the use of "singlets," words that appear only once in the Bible and whose meanings are doubtful. More manuscripts might offer clues to additional usages. And as language itself changes, new translations are needed to make sure everyone can understand the Bible.

While this is of great import to scholars, the average person cares not one whit. However, people do ask what translation they should use. Since most of us are looking for help in our prayer life and are not pursuing scholarship, I think the rule for buying shoes applies to buying a Bible. Try it on and see if it fits. Choose two or three favorite passages from scripture and read them in several translations.

Many Bibles come with introductory essays, explanatory notes, and maps, all aids that once were shunned but which make our understanding easier. Whatever choice you make, it should "fit" you.

It is difficult to find words to describe God, who is front and center in this biblical library. The Bible's human authors fall back on figures of speech and models from their culture. For example, in periods when they are smarting under the strong hand of a conqueror, they dream of a God who will annihilate their enemies, and so he becomes the warrior God. In periods of peace, he is the patriarch of the human clan, paternalistically watching over each member. Among the rural folk, he is a shepherd, and in the Song of Solomon, Solomon even dares to see him as the pursuing lover who cannot take "no" for an answer.

The writers consistently view their God as interacting in their lives, caring about such mundane things as what they eat and what they wear. This God lives among them in a tent when they are wanderers, and acquires a permanent home in the Temple when they become a fixed people. This literary device is called "anthropomorphism," that is, attributing human qualities to a being who does not have them. It brings God very close to his people and allows them to see him as caring deeply about what they do and what they endure.

Our cultural unfamiliarity with all of this is a huge issue. Parts of the Old Testament depict customs and mindsets that are millennia old, and very hard to understand. The next two chapters might help with that.

The great biblical law codes are also culturally specific. Law has to adjust to life. With many new cultural and political developments, new laws counter the negatives that emerge. For example, until cars became a daily part of life, there were no speed limits on our roads.

A biblical example might make this even clearer. As long as the Israelites were slaves in Pharaoh's Egypt, their wretched lives offered few choices. Then comes Moses, with a liberation that brings them to a new land where most of them become farmers. This new life requires new rules for sowing and reaping, skills with which they might be aided by pagan neighbors. However, because they see themselves as God's people, these laws are usually prefaced by "the Lord said." One does not have to imagine an audible voice here. One does have to recognize that the Israelites see themselves as different because their God is different.

They have no need of a goddess of fertility to make their corn abundant nor rituals of magic to press their grapes. They do have a God to thank, a God who created all that lives and grows on this earth. Therefore, they will not reap to the edges of their fields. That crop is for the poor, those who do not have fields of their own, but whose dignity is preserved by laws that allow them to work for what they need.

This early record of God's people tells the entire history of those who were the human ancestors of Jesus. Jesus heard these stories from Mary and Joseph. He read them, as soon as he was of age, in the tiny Nazareth synagogue, and he quoted from them in his public teaching.

We must continue to explore this relation between Old and New Testaments, but in summary, we know we are not being asked for a literal reading. We are being challenged to seek the same great truths that our biblical ancestors sought. Is there a God? Is there a moral code that makes us humans different from the animals? What role do our own choices play in our fate? Since life involves a journey we share with others, what does that require of us?

"Not everyone who is Christian sees the Bible like that, do they?"

You're right. There is indeed another school of religious thinking that so many adhere to — fundamentalism. It is an issue that has arisen in every denomination and faction within Christianity, Judaism, and Islam. Let's begin close to home and then look a bit farther afield.

Christian fundamentalism is uniquely American in its origins. The splits created in many denominations by the Civil War and the erosion of Christian beliefs created by World War I were intensified by the hedonism of the 1920s. All this anxiety was fueled by the new idea of "modernism," which was echoing across the Atlantic from the work of some German biblical scholars.

These scholars, using a deep study of both biblical languages and archeological discoveries, had begun to reassess some biblical texts. They pointed out, for example, that more than one human hand had clearly contributed to the lengthy book of the prophet Isaiah. Their work seemed to threaten the very foundations of faith for literalists. Where could this lead?

In response, in the early 1920s, two brothers from California, Milton and Lyman Stewart, sponsored a series of religious pamphlets, *The Fundamentals*, which claimed to explain the basics of Christian faith to any reader. The brothers circulated these pamphlets free of charge to interested churches, youth groups, summer camps, YMCAs, and the like.

These tracts gave a literal interpretation of major Bible texts, including those that the Stewarts interpreted as indicating that the End Times were coming soon.

The views of these fundamentalists were given more publicity by the Scopes Trial of 1925, in which a Tennessee law that banned the teaching of evolution found itself at the center of a national media event.

The biblical scholars who had held that all the details in the Bible should not be taken literally were now face to face with their accusers, who had been gathering steam for years. The fundamentalists saw the idea of evolution as the root of all evils in the modern world. The scientists saw the possibility of a new view of creation.

The literalists won at the Scopes Trial, but science seemingly won the larger war.

But the battle being waged over biblical literalism and biblical inerrancy was far from over. These two terms are not identical, although they overlap. The literalists insisted that each Bible verse has no need of interpretation. The Bible says what it means and means what it says. The supporters of biblical inerrancy held that since God is the author of the scriptures, what might seem like inconsistencies must simply be ironed out.

The fundamentalists were literalists, all questions of translations aside. They were staunch in denouncing those earlier scholars who had dared to suggest one consider the backgrounds and personalities of the human authors. They were equally adamant about biblical time: A day is a unit of 24 hours; 40 years is just that and not a generic term for a long time.

History aided them with another preoccupation. As the roar of the 1920s was swallowed up by the Great Depression and the guns of World War II sounded, it seemed very possible that the End Times were near. This belief seems to recur with increasing frequency even today. The End Times might come at a significant moment, such as the beginning of a new century or millennium. They might come when someone finds "clues" as to a possible date.

We have all read of some group willing to sell all of their belongings, to preach a kind of last chance at salvation to passers-by, and then to regroup at a select site to await the cosmic catastrophe. While I do not share this interpretation of the Bible, I do have to admire their energy and dedication.

During one of the last such countdowns, I was cornered at Port Authority Bus Terminal in New York City by an eager disciple who waved his Bible in my face and inquired, "You have two more days until the end. Are you ready?"

Without thinking of anything except the bus I was trying to catch, I declared, "I am."

My interlocutor drew back, astonished, and I escaped. As I did, I reflected that I had spontaneously spoken truth. Since I try to live in the daily presence of God, I doubt I could be very different if the final trumpet were tuning up.

The more rapid the pace of change, the more appealing fundamentalism becomes. Sometimes it seems as if there has never been as much change and in such dizzying directions as we are currently experiencing. Some churches are accused of doing too much to adapt to the new. Others are accused of not doing enough. But fundamentalism continues to grow. Why?

Fundamentalism is clear and simple. One has only to read and live the text of the Bible literally. It is God's word, and it is unambiguous. There is no need for explanation or scholarship. It can be heard and seen over the airwaves and in the media daily. Some of its adherents seem to believe that hanging copies of the Ten Commandments in our courthouses will affect law enforcement. Public excommunications and shunnings will bring the "sinner" to repentance. The examples are numerous. The reward is certainty.

While the fundamentalists are not a political party, they do seek a foothold in an accepted party so that their values can be defended. Many of these values center around family issues, and this is where their defense of patriarchal biblical texts from another era can cause consternation in our modern world.

The fundamentalists support a culture of male dominance and of female subservience. This can lead to interesting moments.

A few years ago, I met a woman to whom, in the course of a conversation about Lent, I offered a little guide to the season that I had written. Her response floored me as she rejected it.

"I can only read things that my husband has approved and, of course, nothing written by a woman."

This occurred in New York City in the 21st century!

Fundamentalism worldwide

It is very easy to see why fundamentalism spreads so rapidly in any culture of male dominance, including in the world of Islam in the Middle East. Globalization offers perspectives other than those that have come from familiar traditions, and the reaction to those new ideas can be to attempt to repress them. In areas where women have little access to education, they also lack other resources. Medical care is absent since they cannot approach male physicians, and their culture forbids the training of females in this role.

This is why the Pakistani Taliban would shoot 15-year-old Malala Yousafzai in the head because she advocated education for girls in her country. The indignation of the Western world not only saved her physical life but also gave her a platform from which she continues to defend her views on what we consider a basic human right.

The belligerent jihad against the West is far from the inner jihad that Mohammed urged. Many in Islam lament the way their faith is wielded as a weapon today. It is worth taking a moment to see where history took a turn that changed everything.

Both science and mathematics were once more advanced in the world of Islam than in medieval Europe. The Crusades, those ill-conceived religious wars, had a positive result in introducing Arabic numbers to Europe and thus facilitating study. The Renaissance would give way to industrial and scientific revolutions that changed history. But the Muslim world missed these moments, and lost ground.

Judaism, too, has struggled with its religiously and militaristically fervid, who have their plans to destroy the two mosques atop the Temple Mount in Jerusalem and to rebuild a Jewish Temple there. Some of them are even attempting to breed a special red heifer that could be sacrificed to purify the site.

The existence of fervent fundamentalists is not confined to any one country or faith tradition. And social media have helped their ideas spread. While the Taliban utters curses against the West, terrorists in other countries clutch their cell phones and advanced weaponry.

Many of us struggle to wrap our minds around honor killings by family members for deeds we do not consider criminal. We find it hard to believe that in some places, divorce can only be male-initiated. We find it hard to believe that in Arab countries, some of whom are our political allies, rape is a crime only if there are four male witnesses.

When it comes to fundamentalism, we must read behind what is said in order to find out what is meant. We have to detect that sometimes an innocent expression like "family values" can be a code word for virulent homophobia or racism. It might mask an unwillingness to support legislation to aid the poor because "They are too lazy to work" or "I did it on my own. Let them do the same." Realize that some fundamentalists are reluctant to work for environmental issues because the coming End Times makes that superfluous.

No matter how you define fundamentalism, look for its traces in your own thinking. Hurricane Sandy sweeps the Eastern seaboard, and I am asked, "Do you think God is saying something?" A heat wave grips the country, and someone opines, "I think we are being punished for — " Inevitably, he fills in that blank with his own ideas.

I would like to think that we each have some "fundamental" values of faith and morality on which to stand. However, I also trust that we can be thoughtful enough not to think that a narrow vision is a safe one.

If we believe in an eternal God and not in a God who only spoke in some dark past, then we cannot take refuge in fundamentalism. My God created thinking people. I believe he goes on challenging us to see how we are to be at home in our newer world. If not, my faith is misplaced.

I am fully aware of the careful footwork required for this task, but that is also why I love the scripture challenge: "The word of God is living and active, sharper than any two-edged sword" (Hebrews 4:12).

~9~

"WHERE SHOULD I BEGIN? THE BEGINNING OF THE BIBLE? ARE THERE PITFALLS?"

ONLY BEGIN at the beginning if you realize that the first 11 chapters of Genesis are a little book in themselves, a glimpse into prehistory. They are attempts to answer the questions: Where did it all begin? What was "once upon a time" like?

There has never been a thinking people on this earth without a creation story, and our biblical ancestors are no different. None of them was around before humankind was made — that is quite obvious — so they imagined what God might have done. In fact, they had two stories!

You can easily see the differences. Genesis 1:1-2:3 is the first of these. It is a glorious poetic rendering of a God who creates everything, item by item, in no rush, and who contemplates each — sun, moon, stars, fish, animals, plants — before pronouncing them "good." There is profound theology here. Their neighbors worshipped most of these parts of creation as deities. The Hebrews say, in effect, "They are only creatures. Our God made them."

As the culmination of this act of creating, we come to the human beings, made almost simultaneously, but made in the very image of the creating God. They are worth more than all the rest combined. They are thinking creatures of a personal, thinking God.

And then God rests, giving an illustration of the Hebrew observance of the Sabbath day, which other ancient peoples did not have.

But a different form of this story also existed among members of other tribes. Even in English translations, God's name is rendered differently. (Check your Bible to see if "God" in Chapter 1 becomes "Lord God" in Chapters 2 and 3.)

There is a different scene and purpose in Genesis 2. Here, a desert people imagines perfect bliss as having once existed in a garden watered by not one but four rivers. The human being is created as a working person from the first moment. He is to till and keep the garden, but his loneliness cannot be assuaged by the company of any other creatures. He "names" them and so knows what they are, but they all fail the test for companionship.

In a daring bit of imagination, God makes the woman from the very being of the man so that she is in no way inferior to him.

They are of the same "stuff." (Some, both fundamentalists and feminists, would like to read this as inferiority, but I don't.) This woman goes on to be the chief character in Chapter 3 with its human exploration of the limits of obedience.

Each of these bits of prehistory investigates important human questions from a time when there are no eyewitnesses to answer them for us. Humanly speaking, the Hebrews know that evil, disguised as good, forever tempts us. As livestock tenders, they are only too aware of their conflicts with city dwellers, so they attribute the building of cities to the descendants of Cain, the first murderer. Misunderstandings and the inability to communicate with neighbors who do not speak their language lead to the story of the Tower of Babel and the origin of multiple languages.

Since nothing quite equals the power and terror of uncontrolled water, and since every nation has experienced this, the Hebrews too have a flood story in the saga of Noah, who sees God wiping clean a sinful world.

And since there is much time to be accounted for, and few stories to fill it, we come to the genealogy, a favorite biblical device for covering time and for claiming that each of these people belongs to the ancestor group. They are not mathematicians, and their own short lives lead them to covet old age. They therefore attribute wildly improbable ages to these figures from the past. When Methuselah, for example, is said to have been 969 years old, this is their way of saying, "Time passed by."

These first 11 chapters of Genesis are neither science nor eyewitness reporting, but they are what the original authors intended them to be — clear belief statements about human origins.

The fact that this origin story is not literally true should not diminish its importance. The theology is so vital that Israel put it at the very beginning of its record of how God acted toward them.

We can summarize some of these truths. All creation comes from a caring God who intends human beings to live in harmony while working in this world. Human curiosity and pride lead to disobedience, and evil enters the scene. There can be no going back to what was. Men and women will have to use their intelligence as they make their way across this world. The forces of nature are powerful but not totally obliterative. Humans might have difficulty understanding each other, but that, too, is part of living and roaming. Having laid down these basics, Genesis is ready to take us into "real time," into the world of the first human upon whom we can put an approximate date.

From what today we would call southern Iraq, then known as Ur of the Chaldees, Abraham steps forth in response to a call from his God to "go." He carries with him some of the culture of his origins since he is roughly contemporary with the drawing up of the great Code of Hammurabi. We are now ready to walk into the 19th century B.C.

We cannot leave these earliest chapters of Genesis without one further explanation of a term often used to describe them: "myth." As used here, it is an attempt to find words for a truth that eludes history but is part of the worldview of a culture.

Whether we come from faith or from science, we agree that there was a beginning. At some moment, there has to have been a first man and a first woman. The Bible apparently chooses to name them from their nature. Adam comes from the Hebrew word for "red" since it is a word related to the red earth into which all bodies return. Eve seems to derive from the root for "living," although this is disputed.

A final thought must be added here on the Bible and science. There need be no quarrel between scientists and biblical scholars, since each is working in a different realm. The Hebrews were not a scientific people. They did not sit around their campfires debating evolution. However, there is nothing in these rich presentations of their beginnings that is contradictory to anything that science might offer today.

Evolution, fact or not, still awaits the final links. It could be the way that God chose to create. However, the Bible is not a handbook of science, nor was it intended to be. We err if we try to see it as such.

Shall we give the last word to Paul, a long-time student of the early scriptures?

All scripture is inspired by God and is useful for teaching, for reproof, for correction, and for training in righteousness, so that everyone who belongs to God may be proficient, equipped for every good work. (2 Timothy 3:16-17)

~10~

"I HAVE SO LITTLE KNOWLEDGE OF THE WORLD IN WHICH THE BIBLE IS SET. COULD I HAVE A THUMBNAIL SKETCH, PLEASE?"

THIS MIGHT BE a bit like attempting to write the alphabet on the head of a pin, but there are certain general lines that can make a biblical adventure so much easier to follow. Just keep saying to yourself, "These are real people, with human hopes and fears, and, like me, they live in a world with specific customs."

To step almost anywhere into the Old Testament is to find a tribal, patriarchal world. Every woman has to be under the care of a male, first of her father and then of her husband, just as every male has to belong to the family and its larger unit, the tribe. In these unbreakable bonds are found security and safety. The family is the employment office, the marriage bureau, the source of health care and retirement benefits, the police department, and beyond. No one wants to be an "outsider" because that way lies insecurity. (This still prevails in tribal societies today, a fact our politicians ignore at their peril.)

Sons are highly prized because the father's name is attached to them. For example, Joshua, as son of Nun, is forever linked to a father figure who is thus never lost to memory.

In an agrarian society, children are free labor and are therefore highly valued. Early ideas about biology also contributed to this custom of prizing the male since early peoples believe that the male semen is the sole factor in creating human life. The woman's womb is only a receptacle for his gift. Therefore, if intercourse does not result in a child, it is obviously her fault for having an unreceptive womb, and she is labeled "barren." It took us until beyond the Middle Ages to begin to modify this viewpoint.

Life expectancies are much shorter in these ancient times, and while women begin childbearing at quite young ages, many of them are dead by their early 30s. Men might have an additional decade to live. Long life is always viewed as a gift from God. It is for this reason that the early books of the Old Testament give unimaginable ages to the heroes of Israel.

For generations, this tribal group is a wandering, shepherding people with no fixed abode. After Joseph is sold into slavery in Egypt by his brothers, however, the rest of the clan finds its way there in a time of famine. Joseph's skills are utilized by the Pharaoh, and he provides for his family. But a later Pharaoh who "did not know Joseph" enslaves the descendants of Israel.

The story of their liberation under Moses is the key intervention of God in their history. That interminable journey across the Sinai wilderness is always referred to as "40 years," the Hebrew term for "a long time." They need this time to begin to have a sense of self as a people.

Here is where Moses plays the roles of lawgiver, cheerleader, general, and almost everything else. His task is not an easy one, and there are times of deep discouragement.

Once the people enter the Promised Land, many of them become farmers and so they look to a "judge" for governance, a role that is both religious and political. But the "conquest" of the land is never fully accomplished, so they always have enemies from within and from neighboring countries. By the 11th century B.C., Israel decides to appoint a king to be like every other nation. Her unique existence as a theocracy with God as the ultimate authority comes to an end just before the year 1000 B.C.

The last judge, Samuel, in a far-seeing speech in 1 Sam. 8:11-18, points out the dark side of this choice, but the people are adamant. They want a king, and so the monarchy begins, which will last for more than 400 years. Its glory days are under David, the second king, and under his son, Solomon. David, politically astute though morally questionable, manages to unite all the northern and southern tribes with a capital city, Jerusalem. Situated on the hill-top of Mount Zion (Sion), Jerusalem belongs to no tribe.

This fragile unity collapses under Solomon's son Rehoboam, who inherits a dissatisfied country from his father. Solomon had required labor from his people for the building of the Temple. It is given readily for that purpose. It is given less gladly for Solomon's own palace, and it becomes a burning issue as Solomon multiplies foreign queens. More forced labor is required to build temples for the women's pagan deities. Resentment naturally begins to brew.

Rehoboam turns a deaf ear to the cries of the unhappy people. In the ensuing revolt, the country splits into the richer, more fertile northern kingdom of 10 tribes, now called Israel, and a poorer southern portion, Judah. But tiny Judah has the Temple and the Ark of the Covenant. Since most of the recorded history comes from this latter group, we do have a skewed story that favors the southern tribes.

We have to keep in mind that these people never live in isolation. They are part of the history of the world that swirls around them. By the eighth century B.C., the most militaristic empire in the history of the world is on the move. This is Assyria, with its capital at Nineveh, whose ruins are found today in northern Iraq.

Assyria rumbles across the Mideast, heading for access to the Mediterranean and then for Egypt. On the way, it conquers and subjugates all in its path. Assyria's method is to displace the people of a conquered land and to replace them with other exiles who find themselves unable to rebel in a strange land where they must scramble to earn a living or starve.

By 721 B.C., the inhabitants of Israel are marched away into oblivion by the Assyrians. These 10 "lost tribes" have never been relocated. The foreigners who are brought in to replace them intermarry with the few who remain and become the much-hated Samaritans of later history.

Jerusalem should have become uneasy as the Assyrian behemoth moves with seeming impunity, but a certain self-satisfaction invades the thinking of its inhabitants. They have God's house, the Temple. Surely God will not allow anything to happen to that. In vain do the prophets inveigh against this mindset. In vain do the last kings strip the Temple treasury of its wealth to bribe the enemy. It is too little, too late, since Assyria has also lost its footing, and a mighty new enemy has conquered it. Babylon is now flexing its muscle across the Fertile Crescent.

Babylon cannot abide the arrogance of a hilltop Jerusalem as the sole defiant trifle in its vast new empire. The prophet Jeremiah sees the inevitable end and hides the Ark of the Covenant to protect it from the moment when the Temple will be invaded. (He does a splendid job, since no one has ever redis-covered it!)

Babylon does what no other enemy has done. It destroys the Temple and depopu-lates Jerusalem. In the year 587 B.C., we be-gin the Babylon Exile.

God of the Diaspora

Dismal as the image of a ruined Jerusa-lem may be, this period of exile is of enor-mous importance for the theological growth of Israel. Far from home, the people begin to bring together their scattered stories of God's goodness to them despite their fail-ures. Most scholars agree that an important compiling of the Word of God occurs at this time.

In exile, the Jews realize that they do not need to go to Jerusalem to find God. He is available everywhere in his Word. God is no longer perceived as located in a particular land, but can be found wherever someone is attempting to remember that Word. The exiles, therefore, do not have to go home again to be in God's presence. The Diaspora, the scattering of the Jews around the Mediterranean world, begins.

Some 40 years later, a tolerant Cyrus of Persia subdues Babylon and permits those who are willing to return to Jerusalem. The Temple is rebuilt, but from this time on, Jews can be found all around the world. Their faith and their customs travel with them. Their belief in one God holds firm as they live and work among pagan neighbors, because their daily lives are ordered by their beliefs.

The last centuries before the birth of Jesus are marked in world history by the dazzling conquests of Alexander the Great and the division of his vast empire among his generals at his death. A brief century of Jewish independence under the Maccabees will precede the arrival of imperial Rome, and the position of the eagle over a subservient Palestine.

To understand the Bible, we need to keep in mind that Alexander brought his language with him everywhere he conquered. Greek displaced Aramaic, which had been the universal language during the centuries of Assyrian and Babylonian domination. The language shift is the reason that Greek is used in the last books of the Old Testament period, and the reason those books are later rejected by both Protestants and Jews. We call these books the Old Testament Apocrypha, and they are omitted from most Protestant Bibles. The Apocrypha includes parts of Daniel and Esther, Tobit, Judith, Wisdom, Sirach, Baruch, and 1,2 Maccabees.

The theological growth of the Israelites during these centuries is enormous. They first view their God as territorially bound, belonging to their land. To go to a foreign country was to find another deity in charge there. Hence the custom of shaking loose dirt from one's sandals at border crossings. It is giving back the land that belongs to the local god.

Little by little, but especially during that Exile in Babylon, the Jews come to see that their God is mobile and universal, able to travel with them as long as his Word is alive and well among them. This great truth is why the Bible is so important. The presence of God is there.

Symbolically, the fact that the rebuilt Temple has no Ark of the Covenant is a stark reminder of this. The Jews will continue to go to Jerusalem in pilgrimage until its destruction in 70 A.D., but the veiled Holy of Holies shields only emptiness and memories.

Calendar Dating

The ancients did not have a universal calendar. Important moments were linked to a certain year in the reign of the ruler of the moment. (Read Luke 3:1-2 for a look at how complex this could be.)

As Christianity spread through the Roman Empire, people began to say that the coming of Christ was the dawn of a new era that needed to be noted. In the 6th century of our era, a monk named Dionysius Exiguus (which translates as "Dennis the Small") was given the monumental task of compiling the reigns of emperors and governors to establish the year of Jesus' birth. This would then be called Anno Domini, the Year of the Lord, the great dividing line of history.

Dennis did his best on what must have been an incredible chore. He came up with a year that the authorities then adopted as the commencement of this new time, and all was recalculated.

Much later, someone redid his calculations and found an error. By Dennis's reckoning, Herod the Great died in the year 4 B.C. From the Gospel accounts, Jesus was born before that death, therefore somewhere between 7 and 4 B.C. One can only imagine how both religious and civil officials received this unwelcome discovery. It was decided that it was too late to make another correction. We continue to have a calendar in which Jesus is born B.C. — Before Christ!

In a largely Christian scholarly world, these abbreviations, A.D. and B.C., caused no difficulty, but they leave out scholars of other faiths. For this reason, you will now often find references, in publications that are attempting to be more inclusive, to dates as C.E., the Common Era, and B.C.E., Before the Common Era.

Since all this is ancient history, you might ask: Why bother? Why not skip the Old Testament and focus on the stories of Jesus and his early followers? I say we need to bother for several reasons. First, these are the stories that Jesus was taught in his family circle. These are the foundations of the faith of his people. Second, these portraits of human beings, both good and bad, can give courage to each of us. They are a wonderful reminder that God never expects perfection of any human being, but he does expect effort.

The incredible humanity of some of these heroes is encouraging to those of us who have moments both good and grim on our own paths through life. In studying those who went before, we realize that God does not always work miracles to extract good people from danger and misery, nor does God answer every prayer as the petitioner has dictated it.

I do not subscribe to the theory that everything in the Old Testament foreshadows the New. These events are the consequences of human beings making choices, some good, some less so. We are willing to admit this as we study other figures of world history. Why not do the same for these people who stand as part of the foundation of the three monotheistic religions — Judaism, Christianity, and Islam?

~11~

"I THINK I KNOW MORE ABOUT THE NEW TESTAMENT, BUT I WONDER — ARE THERE ANY RED FLAGS THERE?

SINCE THE GOSPELS are the most-read parts of the New Testament, let's start with a few reminders about them and the world we find there.

Jesus is a first-century Palestinian, something we should never forget. He grows up in Nazareth, then a tiny village in the northern part of the country called Galilee. No one really wants to come from there, since the natives speak with a readily identifiable accent. Because Galilee shares a border with Syria, non-Jews frequently move in, thus tainting the purity of Judaism. This leads to its nickname, "Galilee of the Gentiles."

Life is hard in Galilee, and the vast majority of those who work the land are doing so for absentee Roman landlords. A number of parables are set against this background. Jesus is raised by Mary and Joseph, very probably in an extended household of other relatives. Joseph is referred to as a *tekton*, not quite accurately translated as "carpenter." He is more in the line of a construction worker. It is certainly possible that Joseph and a young adult Jesus would have had ready work in the building of Herod's new city, Sepphoris, a few miles from Nazareth.

Jerusalem lies far to the south, almost a hundred miles away. It is separated from Galilee by the unfriendly province of Samaria, a remnant of that eighth century B.C. resettlement by Assyria. Its mixed population of Hebrews and pagans has evolved its own set of beliefs on the fringes of Judaism. They do not look kindly on groups of Jews traveling to Jerusalem for festivals, above all since their own temple was destroyed by Jerusalem Jews two centuries earlier. (Memories are long in the Mideast.)

Jesus is late in beginning his ministry, and he largely confines it to the towns and villages of Galilee, with a few trips to Jerusalem. We find him most often in the region surrounding that large inland lake known as the Sea of Galilee or Lake Tiberias. From these shores, he calls his first fishermen disciples, and he adopts one of these seaside towns, Capernaum, as his base of operations. Farmers and fishermen are his primary audience and he rarely travels across the lake to pagan territory or north into Tyre and Sidon.

It is a limited yet public world. Family life dominates in these towns, and Jesus almost certainly has grown up surrounded by extended family. By this time in history, polygamy has disappeared, but the support and interaction of family members is still vital to survival. Our modern nuclear family would have been seen as a poor substitute for the richness of having many hands available.

Even in Galilee, Rome cannot be ignored. The tax collectors are everywhere, and Roman soldiers have the right to demand that this conquered people serve them. Soldiers can be found at the mile posts, those markers of a thousand paces. Anyone could be forced to carry a soldier's gear to the next post, but no further. (This is the background for Jesus' wry suggestion to go the "extra mile" if asked [Matt. 5:41]. What a way to mentally disarm the conqueror.)

On the Sabbath day, the synagogue is the place to find the men of the village, for a gathering that is part town meeting and part religious service. Jesus is faithful to these gatherings where a Torah scroll is passed by turn among the attendees for reading and an impromptu commentary.

Jesus does not marry, and that might have made him stand out, since a number of his disciples are married. Peter undoubtedly is, since we know that he has a mother-in-law (Mark 1:30).

Everyone works hard from sunrise to sunset, but the Sabbath day of rest, that uniquely Jewish observance, is a blessed relief. It is indeed a day to celebrate that one is no longer a slave.

Women do not play a large role in public life, and contemporary scholars doubt that synagogue attendance is on their calendar. Thus, the appearance of a woman, and a sick woman, at one of these meeting places can be a cause for speculation among the men gathered there (Luke 13:10-17).

This raises the issue of illness and evil spirits. Medical knowledge in Jesus' time is more limited than ours, and germs are unheard of. If one has a headache, it obviously comes from an evil spirit pounding away in there. The same reasoning applies to intestinal disorders, sprained limbs, and almost anything that medical science cannot handle. While I believe that demonic possession does exist, we must be careful of assuming it widespread.

Mary Magdalene, for example, who is described as having seven demons (Luke 8:2), is almost certainly a very ill woman who is healed by Jesus. "Demon" is not a term used by the Bible to describe sinfulness. Mary is not the village prostitute, despite the Renaissance art that so depicts her. Today we would speak of a biblical "demon" as a virus, a mental illness, or a chronic condition such as arthritis.

For major festivals such as Passover, there might be a pilgrimage to Jerusalem, a long journey of many days on roads made safer by a large number of pilgrims. Since one's outer cloak is a ready bedroll, and since Passover is a springtime festival, that journey can be a pleasant camping trip.

Passover

The central feast of the Jewish calendar and, by extension, of the Christian one, is the celebration of Passover, which helped to define the nature of Israel.

Passover is the joyous festival celebrating freedom from the slavery of Egypt as the Jews fled the Pharaoh and pursued the promise of a new land. While we are not certain about the specific details of the ancient festivities, certain elements seem to have been included from the beginning.

It is a celebration held within the family, either alone or in combination with the nearest neighbors if one's relatives are not sufficient to fill the table and to consume the lamb. The book of Exodus (Ch. 12) specifies that there is to be an explanation given to the children so they will understand why this meal is so important.

The book of Joshua records that one of the first things the Israelites do after entering the Promised Land is to celebrate the Passover (5:10-2). It will be a long time before a central sanctuary is established in Jerusalem. However, when that happens, a pilgrimage to that site becomes part of the ritual, if it is at all possible. Much later, when the dispersion across the Mediterranean world has taken place, the ideal of one day celebrating in Jerusalem becomes part of the ritual.

In the beginning, it seems that the head of the household was responsible for slaughtering the animal. Later, with the centralizing of worship, the Temple priests become involved.

We do not know how it happened, but there seems to have been a long period when Passover was not celebrated.

2 Kings 23:21-23 notes that no such feast "had been kept since the days of the judges in Israel." This would mean that its memory had been lost for more than six centuries. King Josiah's attempt to restore it was resisted by his people. The renewal of fervor after the Babylonian Exile brings it back into prominence and it is certainly again central in the lifetime of Jesus.

This brings us to the images of the Last Supper that have come to us from Christian art of the Renaissance. These images suggest that it was a meal for just Jesus and the 12 disciples. If it were a true Passover, where are the female disciples and those faithful others who had followed Jesus all the way from Galilee to Jerusalem?

The Gospel texts are not clear as to who attended. Certainly the 12 were there, but we are left to wonder who did the cooking — these fishermen?

Bohdan Piesecki, a contemporary artist, has painted a delightful and possibly more accurate Last Supper, with men and women at the table and an assortment of squirming children celebrating, too.

We all might need to rethink our ideas here, since the scriptures are quite clear that the women and other disciples are part of the Upper Room community through the rest of that weekend. And it does seem impolite to have barred them from this final meal with Jesus, who was fed by their effort during those previous months on the road.

To this day, Jews across the world make every effort to celebrate this feast in a family setting. Since the death and rising of Jesus are tied to Passover time, Christians are forever linked to their Jewish brothers by it. We are all blessed in those years when lunar and solar calendars converge so that we remember our common story together on the very same days.

In daily life, most activities in Jesus' world would have taken place outside, because houses are tiny. The courtyard of a house becomes the extension of the living quarters with little privacy or secrecy. Jesus is always in the public eye. He can honestly say, "I have said nothing in secret. Why do you ask me? Ask those who heard what I said to them; they know what I said" (John 18:20-21).

This province of Palestine has a Roman procurator, a job that turns over with some regularity. Rome has also installed local rulers in the persons of Herod the Great and his family. This choice rankles with many Jews since the Herodian dynasty is not truly Jewish. Its members come from an Idumean tribe that adopted Judaism with an eye to the future. That plan has been solidified by their currying favor with Rome. Rome finds them useful; the Jews despise them since their religious practice is only for show.

Who was Jesus?

Jesus is born at the very end of the reign of Herod, who has undertaken a vast embellishment of the Temple area to impress the Jews with his devotion. It is his son, Herod Antipas, who will order the execution of John the Baptist, and it is he to whom Jesus scornfully refers as "that fox" (Luke 13:32).

Jesus is not about to propose the overthrow of Rome. He is not a political revolutionary, contrary to the views of some modern critics. Nor is he in a position to upend the whole social structure of that empire. He is a Jewish teacher, well versed in the story of his people and determined to show that the current religious leadership, too involved in toadying to Roman power, has lost its way.

Reza Aslan

Jesus once asked, "Who do you say that I am?" and people of every background have gone on responding since then. In his recent book *Zealot*, scholar Reza Aslan becomes the latest of these answerers.

Aslan suggests that Jesus is the man of his title, a failed political revolutionary who gathered an army of disciples with the goal of establishing an earthly kingdom that would replace Caesar with God. In his efforts, Aslan reads some of the Gospels literally and some not, but it seems that he has missed the heart of the story.

This idea of an overtly political Jesus is an old chestnut that has long since been roasted to death by scholars. Jesus' disciples were never an army in any militaristic sense. The only time Peter wielded a sword, he managed to do nothing but slice off the ear of a servant! Jesus never defied authority in the persons of the occupying Romans. He stated loudly and clearly, "My kingdom is not of this world."

Aslan makes much of the lack of literacy among the followers of Jesus. To many moderns, illiteracy is synonymous with ignorance. However, in an oral society, the power of the spoken word and of memory is where history is to be found. Unless reading materials are widespread, literacy is not a universal value.

Saddest of all, Aslan turns Paul into a loose cannon, at odds with James and Peter, preaching a different faith from that held by the Jerusalem church. I have to cry "foul" here. Paul, a well-educated rabbi, was at pains to find a way to welcome Gentile believers into a faith that he held was rooted in his own cherished Judaism, a first-century Judaism that was no more monolithic than it is today.

Paul would die long before any Christian break with the synagogue would become final. Aslan misses the vital point that Roman law recognized Judaism as a legitimate religion, which gave its practitioners legal rights. These would not be lightly tossed away by The Way, which was widely perceived as another branch of Judaism until about the year 90 A.D.

Finally, Aslan never really addresses why people of faith would have continued to turn to this failed political revolutionary, if that is all he was, for light and inspiration over the past 2,000 years. If Aslan is right, this rebel's words should have died with his ambitions on Calvary. They did not. Why?

Jesus sees both Pharisees and Sadducees as at fault for providing poor religious leadership to Judaism. A word about each of these groups might help in understanding certain Gospel passages.

The high priests, whose domain is the Jerusalem Temple, belong to the party of the Sadducees. They cling to the Torah, the first five books of the Bible. They want nothing to disturb their status with the Romans, who appoint them after appropriate bribes have been paid.

The Pharisees, on the other hand, are primarily active outside Jerusalem in the towns and villages where the synagogues anchor religious life. Once the Word of God becomes a written document in the sixth century B.C., that Word has to be interpreted. The Pharisees are the self-appointed guardians of that law, but some of them have become overzealous. They have taken the gift of those 10 basic commands to Moses and have parsed them into 613 precepts. Their intentions are good; their suspicions are not. Jesus will often be forced to condemn the resulting legalism that is not life-giving.

Each of these groups, Pharisees and Sadducees, has its own scribes and lawyers. Since Jesus has studied with none of the recognized rabbis of the day, they are heard to ask, "How does this man have such learning when he has never been taught?" (John 7:15).

They are also incensed by the methods Jesus uses. Ordinarily, one becomes a rabbi by walking with one, with no more than two disciples to a teacher. When these two have memorized all that the rabbi knows, they are ready to separate and acquire their own disciples. Jesus doesn't do this. He has a large, unwieldy band of followers, and he encourages them to ask questions. (Just studying these questions is a wonderful way to reflect on what Jesus thinks is important.)

This is an outdoor, pushing-and-shoving kind of discipleship, with much public life and few quiet moments. We can understand why Jesus arises early in the morning to go off by himself to pray, or why he tries occasionally to have some quiet time with those he is preparing to carry on his work.

One way we might experience this in our own prayer life is to go to a Gospel and choose an incident. Read the story carefully and try to imagine yourself part of that crowd. (There is always room for one more.) Listen to what Jesus says. Watch how he acts. For example, in a moment of healing, does he touch the person? Why or why not? In this male-dominated, paternalistic world, how does he treat the women?

This last is not an idle question. Feminists have come down hard on both sides of the question of whether Jesus was a feminist. In our modern use of the term, he belongs to neither party. But in the first-century world, he opens wide a door for women becoming part of the inner circle of disciples. No other rabbi would have permitted a woman to listen and to learn as he does.

As you read, ask yourself how he speaks to those who come to him. Does he use family terminology like "brother" or "daughter"? Does he use that untranslatable "woman"? We must note that in Jesus' day, it is a term of the utmost respect, which he uses for his own mother on Calvary (John 19:26). It is best rendered as something like "honored lady."

It is probably safest to say that Jesus waves the flag of no religious faction, conservative or liberal. He comes as the living word spoken into a world hungry for hope. This is what he offers to his contemporaries.

The Gospels

There was no one recording the words and deeds of Jesus as they happened. There was no need to, since the witnesses could repeat the stories for those not present. After Jesus left this world, the disciples were convinced he would return in glory soon, and this earth would cease as they knew it. So nothing needed to be written.

Then, little by little, they begin to realize that Jesus is not returning in their lifetime. Something has to be done so that the story not be lost. They create a literary form that is new, something they call a "gospel." That word means "good news," and that is the perspective they offer.

Most scholars agree that the Gospels were assembled backwards. That is, the death and resurrection were written first because they were the most important parts. Later, some of the teachings and actions of Jesus were added to these foundational texts. Two of these authors — Luke and Matthew — would complete their Gospels by appending a nativity story at the beginning, in the style of the first-century world.

As we moderns look at the Gospels, we are often disappointed. The kinds of details that we would love to have are not there, nor do we have much information about the authors. We have the four names that have long been given to them, but it seems more than probable that these cloak the fact that one or more of the early communities pooled their memories for the final product.

Using the names commonly attributed to them, let's take a look at the individuality of each Gospel.

Mark's Gospel is believed to be the first one written. It is a rather terse account of a Jesus who stirs recognition among the evil spirits, but who meets with unbelief from his own people. His brief, clear record serves as a guide for Matthew and Luke.

Matthew's narrative, thought to have originated in the Jewish-Christian community at Antioch in Syria, is directed to a similar first-century audience. It portrays Jesus as a new Moses, teaching as his ancestor did, but amplifying his teachings for a new time. The fidelity of Jesus to his Jewish roots is very apparent.

By contrast, Luke's audience is the vast pagan world where, as companion of Paul on his travels, the author has lived and taught. Luke's good news emphasizes the outreach of Jesus to outsiders. His parables such as the Good Samaritan, and his narratives with their emphasis on the women disciples and on the table fellowship that Jesus shares with those seen as outcasts, are a unique indication that Jesus has a message for the wider world.

John's Gospel was composed long after these first three, possibly at the beginning of the second century A.D. It is almost as if the author says, "Now is the time to reflect more deeply as the message of Jesus is being challenged by very divergent views." He offers a soaring theological reflection on the Word made flesh. His opening words, "In the beginning," take one back to the first verse in Genesis. The coming of Jesus is seen as the new creation. John does not hesitate to depict Jesus confronting the religious leaders of his day. Unfortunately, many in later eras have failed to recognize that when the author says "the Jews," he is referring to the entrenched bureaucracy in Jerusalem. Misunderstanding this has led to John's Gospel being the basis for much anti-Semitism. Jesus, as a Jew, could not be anti-Semitic. The Jews were his own people.

By the end of the second century, these four accounts are established as the authentic ones. But others are circulating as well, some of which attempt to fill in the blank spaces with such wonderfully fanciful tales as that of the child Jesus making mud pie birds that miraculously take life and fly away! Others fill in the life of Mary and Joseph, or support some divergent view of the nature of Jesus. These "unofficial" stories are almost like religious novels.

In short, each Gospel writer fashions his material to fit the faith story he wants to portray. There is no attempt to be terribly careful about times and places. None of that is important. What Jesus says and does is the crucial thing.

All of the Gospel writers have their own strengths. Mark seems made for us moderns in a hurry since his is the briefest account. Luke is appealing to those of us who are non-Jews because he often explains Jewish customs. Matthew's is the clearest portrait of Jesus the teacher, and John gives us a series of individuals who are transformed by meeting Jesus. Try them all!

12

"BUT THE GOSPELS AREN'T ALL THERE IS, ARE THEY? ISN'T THERE MORE IN THE NEW TESTAMENT?"

YOU ARE ABSOLUTELY RIGHT. While the Gospels appear first in all our New Testaments, they actually are almost the last part to have been written. However, since the coming of Jesus is the focus of the New Testament, the Gospels have to come first.

The book that directly follows the Gospels provides exciting answers to the question, "And then what happened?" It comes to us in the book named the Acts of the Apostles, which is volume two of Luke's Gospel. (Read the opening verses of both, and this will be obvious.) Acts is colored by reminiscences from those "good old days." It chronicles the first decisions and trials of the followers of Jesus as they try to bring the Good News to their world.

Acts depicts these followers' outreach, first to their own world at a time when there is no contradiction in speaking of Jewish Christians. It also, with a bit of a rosy glow, shows the first attempts at community living, and then the mission to the vast pagan world of the Roman Empire. Once Paul appears on the scene, he usurps the spotlight and we journey with him across provinces criss-crossed by Roman roads.

The fact that Paul dominates so much of Acts is largely due, scholars think, to the fact that the author of Acts — Luke — is both companion and personal physician to Paul, who was plagued by a recurring physical problem, possibly malaria. Since Luke knows Paul best, he writes of his work in preaching the Christian message, called "the Way," to the provinces of Asia Minor and on into Europe. It is a dynamic, very human story of successes and failures. Almost nothing in literature ranks with the pulsing drama of the storm at sea in Chapters 27 and 28. Lord Nelson is reported to have read them the night before the Battle of Trafalgar.

This brings us to what ranks among the best-known parts of the New Testament, the letters of Paul. They have probably been more read and preached upon than the Gospels themselves, and we need to wave a big red flag before moving on.

Paul wrote these letters. That is, he dictated them to scribes so that they might go out to the fledgling house churches he was establishing anywhere that a Roman road might lead. In every instance, he is responding to specific problems in these communities. While his letters can be profoundly inspirational for us today, we have to keep in mind that they are not universal mandates. Paul is not writing to us. We are reading someone else's mail without full knowledge of either the situations or the personages involved.

In addition, Paul is evolving in his thinking and in his theology. He never personally met Jesus nor heard the Lord's teaching first-hand. There is no handbook of Christianity, so it is only natural that Paul is often groping for ways to express what he is experiencing.

The earliest of his letters, I Thessalonians, seems to indicate that he thinks the End Times are coming soon, an idea he shared with many of the disciples. He modifies that belief before long. Remember, too, that he has been formed as a Jewish rabbi, and his ancestral faith can never be forgotten. Paul's challenge is to find ways to convince a largely pagan audience that Judaism and the Way are totally compatible.

Picturing the writing process can also help us understand Paul. Paul uses secretaries. He is most probably striding up and down, dictating to someone or ones seated with an inkpot on the floor. On occasion, his sentences get tangled. Thoughts begin and then never find their completion. Ideas tumble over each other.

Reading and Writing in the First-Century World

While it seems that many Jewish men could read — the synagogue meetings depended on this — the process of writing was technically complex and limited to expert practitioners known as the scribes.

A scribe needed either parchment or papyrus, a quill pen, and ink that was a carbon derivative. He also needed a kind of glue or gum to fasten the ink to the sheet. Crouched on the ground, the scribe could pen three syllables per minute and so write perhaps 72 words in an hour. Each sheet of papyrus held about twice that number of words. A letter as brief as I Thessalonians would require 10 sheets of papyrus.

Given the tediousness of their trade, most scribes worked only two or three hours a day. We can also see why the average person had little need for this skill. In an oral society where word was law, there were relatively few written documents.

Paul wants to share with others what he has come to know. "For I handed on to you as of first importance what I in turn had received..." (I. Cor. 15:3). He uses his energy, his scholarship, and his boundless dreams to do this.

He has most enthusiastic helpers wherever he goes, men whose names appear with his as coauthors of the letters. We also do not have all his letters. We know that he wrote to the Colossians: "And when this letter has been read among you, have it read also in the church of the Laodiceans; and see that you read also the letter from Laodicea" (Col. 4:16). That Laodicean letter has never surfaced. I say this to indicate that we do not have a complete record of Paul's thinking. Perhaps this is the place to note another custom of the first-century world: the "honoree author."

It was not only acceptable but was considered an honor for a disciple to write something as if it had come from the pen of the original person. Take, for example, the letters to Timothy from the New Testament. They speak of situations where the structure of the house churches

has reached a point that overseers or bishops have clearly defined roles. This could hardly have occurred in the decades of the 50s and 60s when Paul is at work.

What could have happened is that some bits of Paul's teachings never got into an official letter. They, plus advice from one of Paul's successors, are blended together in an effort to say: If Paul were alive, this is what he would want us to consider. The original readers fully understand this. They know that Paul is dead and that this is a disciple advising them in his spirit. Most of us don't know this — or at least some of us didn't, until this moment!

Paul, unlike Cephas (Peter) and the other early followers, does not have a wife to encourage him on his unending journeys. He must often have longed for someone besides good friends to share the triumphs and the disappointments of his mission. Read Romans 11 for an insight into his heart, which longs to see his own people find the Jesus whom he has come to know. It is heartbreakingly human.

As difficult as Paul sometimes seems to be, he is among the best educated of the early Christians and one of the first with the background to explain how Christians, a tiny drop in a vast world of paganism, might see themselves. Some of his images will never lose their strength: the Body of Christ to which each of us brings a unique gift for the benefit of all, or believers as clay jars with an inestimable gift within. He also welcomed women into the ministry as teachers and leaders of the house churches. We have so much to be grateful for in the letters that have survived.

The Bible includes also other letters in addition to those of Paul: letters attributed to Peter, James, John, and Jude. These attributions do not always indicate who the author actually was, but we have them because the early Church thought them of value.

Now do I dare to mention that book that concludes the New Testament, the often quoted, frequently decoded Book of Revelation? I stand with the majority of biblical commentators in believing that this book has little to do with the end of our world on a given date and everything to do with encouraging early Christians suffering under the heavy hand of imperial Rome. It is actually a bit like a political cartoon, a commentary on current events.

The author, not wanting to find himself imprisoned, does not dare to directly criticize Rome. Instead, he adopts a favorite Jewish literary form, the apocalypse narrative. The author, exiled to the island of Patmos, begins with seven letters to prominent church communities, citing their moral failures. Then in a wildly imaginative series of scenes, a great battle begins between the forces of evil and the power of God. These scenes match those in any horror movie ever filmed! Good, in the person of the Lamb, triumphs after the final battle.

The author never speaks of Rome. Instead he uses the code word "Babylon" for the evil empire. Every reader from the Jewish world would have known its significance, because it was Babylon, five centuries earlier, that had done what no other enemy of God's people had dared to do. Babylon had destroyed the Temple in Jerusalem.

So the author of Revelation writes for all those suffering persecution from the newest of evil empires, Rome. His message is that this mighty power too will one day "bite the dust," just as Babylon had.

Since this context is far removed from our life today and since the literary form is so unfamiliar, this book is front and center when every natural disaster strikes. The fundamentalists quote from it literally.

Rather than wind ourselves up in those coils, I would recommend that you go to Chapters 21 and 22, two of the loveliest in the Bible. They offer a glimpse of life after suffering, a peering into the heavenly realm that is conceived of as a new Jerusalem. They could only have come from the pen of a homesick Jew to whom all the beauty of the now-vanished earthly Jerusalem would have to be found in the next life. These are exquisite lines, filled with images of light and abundance in the radiant presence of the Lamb. It is no wonder that the final cry of the soul is "Maranatha ... come, Lord Jesus" (Rev. 22:20).

Now does any of this Bible commentary make it seem as if the Bible should still gather dust on a shelf? I hope not. We have not consigned other ancient literature to an eternal resting place. If *The Odyssey* remains the quintessential novel for the questing spirit of every age, and it does, then the Bible is the most complete record we have of a people who want to tell us that they have a God like no other, a God whose work in this world is ongoing.

It is worth our time to delve into this resource and give the human authors time to tell us what the Spirit has impelled them to record. We will never fully fathom the depths of the Bible. I learn something new daily, but every step is an adventure. Go for it!

13

"FAITH IS A LOADED WORD. IT MAKES ME HESITATE."

NOW COMES REALITY. It is one thing to read about a relationship with God. It is something else to actually venture into having one. This is quite simply a gigantic step of faith.

In our world where we interact digitally with so many and personally with so few, faith is venturing into a new realm. I will not deny that, but the effort and its rewards are life-changing. They shake the pillars that hold up a mentality of detachment. We have become so wary of the interpersonal. We fear edging close to anyone, lest we be incapable of meeting that person's needs or they ours. So we recoil from the demands of relationships.

In this realm of a God relationship that we have been discussing, a commitment must be made. God has no email address. I have tried to sell you on the concept of a personal God, a great gift to a world that both yearns for and hesitates before interacting with him.

The serious searcher has to squarely face the issue of who is God. I hold that God is not a remote being, indifferent to the human effort to make sense of life. For too long, religious thinking has kept God firmly on a throne beyond the earthly sphere. For me, the great biblical revelation is that this God invites us into friendship and, yes, into love. "See, I have inscribed you on the palms of my hands" (Isaiah 49:16). That sounds like he cares, doesn't it?

No, we have no right to expect a fairy godmother kind of intervention in which God makes all things right. Yes, the very word "life" implies its opposite. All of nature speaks to us of this, which I'm reminded of as I look out my window at autumn's annual shutting down of nature.

We desperately cling to hopes of pushing human life to the age of 120 or beyond, but reality tells us that there has to be an end to this life at some time. We are not made to tumble into darkness forever. There has to be more; my faith brings me to this. If not, then why bother?

As human beings, we have responsibilities to each other that have to be based on something besides altruism. Some of us have more and some have less, but we all share one gift: life itself. For the person struggling to be a man or woman of faith, the possibilities are endless.

A character in a recent novel I was reading spoke of belief like this: "It's important to believe in something because you can." We can; do we?

Faith is a venture into the unknown. I can only tell you about the joy of a life where God has a place. I cannot do it for you, nor can I give you a taste of its frustrations and its blessings.

I know the mockers who insist that a "pie in the sky" belief in the reality of God is only a way to console ourselves when all does not go well in this world. That is not what true faith is about. Faith rests on the conviction that, to put it bluntly, God would not have gone to all the trouble of revealing something of himself to us only to frustrate us by telling us that our aspirations to know more and to be more are baseless. That sounds too much like a cynical atheism.

No one can deny that physical and moral evils exist. There are no pat explanations for these, although we daily grow in the knowledge that many of them are man-made, as we poison our environment and suffer the consequences. It is much too easy to say that God could fix any or all of them if God existed. But why should he? That kind of childish thinking puts God back into being a mop-up figure whose sole purpose is to be the repairer of human heedlessness. That is not the God I am talking about.

The God of whom I speak has made us to live together on earth with the promise of more to come. It has struck me how inter-related other earthly creatures are with each other. They are scavengers and suppliers for each other, living, foraging, traveling, and migrating in groups or families. The more scientists learn about nature, the more in-triguing it becomes to see the biological community life that exists. By sound and in-stinct, millions of birds migrate annually without technological aid, but with purpose and accuracy.

And we? In isolated singleness, glued to a handheld device, we grope our way forward. Faith says we can do better. Faith says we must do better. Faith that a greater Being has ideas of who we might become, ideas that we strive to understand even as we peel back the layers of who this God is. Knowl-edge like this is both a burden and a gift.

Something happened to me recently at Port Authority Bus Terminal in New York that might illustrate this. I was part of a line that seemingly was on an interminable wait for a bus. There were no seating arrange-ments in the waiting area, but I availed myself of a brick divider between the gates and rested against it.

Along came a young father with a three-year-old child asleep on his shoulder and her doll dangling from his free hand. Instinctively I got up, saying, "Please, you have a burden and could use this seat more than I."

His response? "Carrying love is never a burden."

And so he stood, with a smile, for the next 10 minutes until we finally boarded. It was such an image of trusting love. She was asleep, but she allowed him to hold both her and her most valued possession, that doll, which he kept safe for her so that, an hour later into our trip, when she awoke, I could hear her delighted laughter as they played together with it. Her trust was not misplaced.

Our faith journey can be a similar voyage of love. The exciting part of a loving faith is that we come to God with no fear. We have so misunderstood that phrase "fear of the Lord" from the Bible. In the original Hebrew, it means a respect born of awe, of the desire to be in a right relationship with someone whom we honor. That is part of the discovery of what it means to love God.

We will never feel the same kind of response from God that we might get from our human love of another person, but we are right to use the word *love* because that is what it is.

We are a bit careless in English with the things we "love." That one word takes care of our response to parents, friends, pizza, good movies, chocolate.... One word seemingly fits all, doesn't it? Our heart might not go pitter-patter when we love God, but our faith conviction says he deserves the best we can offer.

So often, religious speakers stress our unworthiness, our failure, or our good efforts gone astray. No one denies the inadequacy of human endeavors, but that is no reason not to try.

A God more loving than that bus-station parent is waiting for us to awaken and enjoy the Divine presence on our journey. So — ?

~14~

"I FEEL AS IF I'M ON THE EDGE OF THE HIGH DIVING BOARD. IF I LAUNCH MYSELF, I MIGHT JUST MAKE A BIG SPLASH!"

WHILE I CAN SMILE at the diving-board image in your question, I'll have to reject it. You do need some skill to perform a dive. But you need no particular technique to begin your spiritual journey. It is much more like standing before a treasure house with the key in your hand. All that is required is to open the door, and it is yours.

I do still want to call it a journey because I guarantee that it will take you somewhere. I am assuming that there is some reason why you keep wondering "Is there more?" The answer has to be "Yes." However, as long as you wait before the door, you will never know what is inside.

In one real sense, our society is never going to help us travelers. All the electronic gadgets in the world — each of which is outdated before you unpackage it at home — each of these promises to do something better, faster, more easily than whatever it was that you had before. That is the natural tagline for selling a product. (Have any of those modern rewriters of the Bible come up with a version of Eve being lured not by fruit but by a new app or iPad?)

To begin to pray or reflect is to consider seriously the *you* within that is too often ignored as we keep putting other people and other goals front and center in our lives.

We are also sometimes diverted by a nostalgic longing for those good old days before modern living got in the way and filled both nights and days. We rue what was lost.

If you can find a nonagenarian, have a talk with him or her. They might challenge you about what you have done with the time saved since the advent of automatic washers and dryers, with the packaged and frozen foods that pushed aside daily grocery shopping, or with the energy saved when one no longer has to shovel coal and clean the ash pit.

I recently lost a centenarian cousin who could remember gas lamps and homes without telephones. It was an "old" world, but how "good" it was she would have debated, since she also loved modern living. We can learn a wonderful lesson from our bodily structure about the dangers of nostalgia. Since I am not an atheist, I do believe in creation, and I stand in awe of the Being who imagined us into life. Just look at yourself.

You have a head that only focuses well by looking forward, feet that move most readily in that direction, and a body that is frontally oriented. To me, this structure says a great deal about where we need to focus.

By all means, let's turn around and check where the past has a lesson to teach. It is only the fool who does the same dumb thing twice. But then, let's turn back to this moment, this day, and celebrate that.

I have not forgotten those 19th-century porters that we left in an African jungle at the beginning of this book. In terms of worldly wealth, they had little. They had even less of scientific know-how and probably almost nothing in terms of a worldview of their civilization.

However, they possessed something that the self-important European explorers had misplaced somewhere during their life journeys. The porters knew they had a soul, a spiritual component that was intimately bound up with their physical being. They could see no point in driving themselves beyond exhaustion just to catch a boat. In their thinking, there would be another some other day. In the meantime, an inner self was crying out to be rested and reunited with a fatigued body. They were wise men.

And here you stand with a dozen excuses and no real reasons. Pick up that imaginary key and give yourself an experience. Commit yourself to prayer time and reflection time for the next two weeks. Be faithfully honest and honestly faithful. Stick with it despite everything that might entice you to abandon the effort.

A spiritual time out

When children get overwrought and overtired, we adults know enough to call for a "time out" for them. Why are we so blind in regard to our own needs? We applaud those who take the time for physical self-care. Is our inner self less important?

You are going to make great discoveries about yourself, your world, and that wonderful seesaw which is life. Up or down, the view is real. We need both perspectives because life is never static.

Some days, just sit in the quiet and let it touch you. I love the story of the elderly woman who used to sit quietly in her church for long periods of time. When asked what she said to God, she replied, "I just look at him and he looks at me."

Keep in mind that prayer is an exercise, requiring repetitions until it becomes as regular for you as rolling out the exercise mat or putting on your shoes. Best of all, it can be done anywhere. On the days you just can't squeeze in a chunk of reflection time, you don't have to lament having no God time that day. Every day has those in-between moments that a prayer can tap. Above all, don't let the day end without at least a nightly sign-off and a "Thanks, God, for what was."

Ready? Turn the key and see what is waiting.

ACKNOWLEDGMENTS

NO BOOK COMES INTO BEING by the author's efforts alone. There are many people whose influence on my life has found its echo in these pages. However, some in particular must be named:

I must confess my huge debt of gratitude to Linda Phillips Ashour, who leavened her persistence that I write this book with some wonderful California hospitality.

Robert Asahina has been an extraordinary editor, as well as a provoker, cheerleader, and visionary, which puts him in a unique category. To say thank you is really inadequate.

I am so grateful to Gabriella Oldham for her incomparable assistance in turning my pages into a manuscript and for her ongoing stimulus.

Catherine Gormley, SU, the cheerful keeper of our digital links and my daily inspiration, is in a category by herself.

Ruth Graham, meticulous copy editor, helped to make the fuzzy clear and the focus firm. I am so grateful.

So many others at Marble Collegiate Church and in my religious community have expressed interest and offered encouragement as well as registering friendly impatience with my pace. I appreciate each of you!

And there are those many, many others in my classes over the years who have asked the questions that sparked these reflections. Please continue to do so, since you enrich me immeasurably!

ABOUT THE AUTHOR

CAROL M. PERRY, SU, is the Resident Bible Scholar at Marble Collegiate Church in New York City. She is the co-author of *Called and Sent* and has been a recipient of two National Endowment for the Humanities grants. She was selected as an Educator of the Year by the Association of Teachers of New York and has lectured across the country on scripture, Christian feminism, and the role of women in the Biblical world. A Sister of St. Ursula, she is a graduate of Fordham University and earned an M.A. in Theology at St. Mary's, Notre Dame.

Sister Carol's blog is at:
http://new.marblechurch.org/Blog/tabid/229/articleType/CategoryView/categoryid/6/Sister-Carol-Perry.aspx

CPSIA information can be obtained at www.ICGtesting.com
Printed in the USA
BVOW07s1721301214

381349BV00001B/18/P